HAUNTED
TERRE HAUTE

HAUNTED
TERRE HAUTE

ASHLEY HOOD

Published by Haunted America
A Division of The History Press
Charleston, SC
www.historypress.com

First published 2019

Manufactured in the United States

ISBN 9781467143714

Library of Congress Control Number: 2019943357

Notice: The information in this book is true and complete to the best of our knowledge. It is offered without guarantee on the part of the author or The History Press. The author and The History Press disclaim all liability in connection with the use of this book.

The boundaries which divide Life from Death are at best shadowy and vague.
Who shall say where the one ends, and where the other begins?

Edgar Allan Poe
"The Premature Burial"

CONTENTS

Acknowledgements

This book would not have been possible without the stories and local folklore that my mother instilled in me from an early age. She would buy me books on ghosts and hauntings, even finding ones made especially for elementary school students when I was very young. As I got older, more books would follow and my fascination with the paranormal grew. As a teenager, she took my friends and me out to local haunted locations, regaling us with the tales associated with the locations and oftentimes looking for the ghosts that remained there. Sadly, my mother passed away in 2011, but I must thank her—if it were not for her, I might not even be writing this book.

I am so very grateful to my friend of twenty-plus years, Elizabeth Christjansen, for taking all of the modern photos in this book and for being willing to venture out to these haunted locations with me in the middle of a frigid Indiana winter. I hope you will photograph more haunted locations for me in the future, but rest assured, I will certainly pick a warmer season the next time around.

Thank you to Sketch Brumfield for always being willing to visit strange and haunted locations with me and for oftentimes being the driver on these adventures. I must also thank you, Elizabeth Christjansen and Vanceletta Colclasure, for listening to many of the stories in this book, probably on several occasions at this point.

I appreciate everyone who shared their stories with me for taking the time to discuss the haunts of Terre Haute. I always love to hear a new version of an old legend, but I also learned some stories that were previously unknown to me. Your input was so helpful in compiling the information for this book. The continued circulation of stories like those contained in this book is key to keeping the history of haunted Terre Haute alive.

An extra big thank-you has to go to Logan Fenimore and the Iota Delta Chapter of Pi Kappa Alpha at Rose-Hulman Institute of Technology. They were so fantastic and helpful with my research for this book. Not only did they supply me with a plethora of useful information, but I was also allowed to visit the site of the former Glenn Home and tour the grounds. All of the photos of the Glenn Home used in this book were also taken at the time of the tour.

Lastly, I must also thank Susan Tingley and the Vigo County Historical Society for allowing me to use vintage photos from their collection, as well as a recent photo of local legend Stiffy Green. The society is keeping the history and the haunts of Terre Haute alive, and for that, we should all be thankful.

INTRODUCTION

Before I visit a haunted location, I like to do as much research as possible. I want to be aware of the activity that I might encounter and to familiarize myself with the spirits known to inhabit the site. I also have a keen interest in the history and architecture of locations and the events that may have contributed to the supernatural energy that remains. I have experienced a variety of strange things in my paranormal investigations, some of which can easily be explained as coincidental or the result of external sounds and activity. However, there have also been many instances when I've experienced something that can only be described as otherworldly. It is those interactions that continue to fascinate me and drive my curiosity about the spirit world and its ghostly residents. Many of the sites contained in this book were the first haunted places that I learned about as a child, so it was important for me to look at the locations from a new perspective and, when possible, to add as much relevant history about the spectral inhabitants of Terre Haute and the locations they call home.

While Terre Haute may at first glance seem like any other quiet Midwest river town, such is not the case. Terre Haute has a rich, albeit sometimes dark, history. It was originally platted in 1816 and would later be incorporated, first as a town in 1832 and later a city in 1853. In the years since, it has been referred to as the "Crossroads of America," the "Paris of Indiana" and "Sin City." All fitting titles for the little city along the Wabash.

Terre Haute's earliest inhabitants were a tribe of Native Americans called the Wea. They chose the area for its proximity to the Wabash River. There was plenty of water available and abundant fish, and the soil was fertile. It was the perfect location for a settlement. Unfortunately for the Wea, they were not the only ones to recognize the benefit of such a location. When the first settlers arrived, they forced the Wea out of their home, taking the land for themselves and naming it Terre Haute, a French term for "High Land." They built meager cabins along the river and lived a hard existence in the wilds of early Terre Haute.

With the founding of Vigo County in 1818, things began to change. Terre Haute started to take advantage of the Wabash River in a different way and prospered with steamboat traffic. The building of the Wabash-Erie Canal increased the water trade even further, and the arrival of railroads put Terre Haute on the map. It was during this time that Terre Haute became one of the biggest pork producers in the nation, allowing Terre Haute to thrive even further. Sadly, that did not last long, as Kansas City and Chicago had started producing pork as well, putting a strain on the established companies in Terre Haute. The city was in dire need of a replacement for the lost industry, but a solution was not far off.

Reserves of iron, coal and oil were found throughout the county and neighboring areas, giving Terre Haute a rich new resource to tap into. Mills and foundries sprang up in the area producing everything from nails to railroad cars. By 1870, Vigo County was once again booming. It was ranked third in the state in coal mining and fifth in manufacturing. A decade later, it ranked fifth in the production of flour and gristmill products and in the production of distilled liquor. Sulfuric waters were also found, and bathhouses were opened to cater to the community.

Workers flocked to Terre Haute for the available work, taking advantage of the new industries at their disposal. However, with so many factories came discourse among the employees. Unions began to form, causing strikes, lockouts and a breakdown of communication between workers and employers.

Terre Haute continued to progress further, adding telephone services and a waterworks, which ushered the city into a new, more modern era. It was during this time that the city gained a reputation as the "Paris of Indiana." The first Terre Haute House, formerly known as the Prairie House, opened at the corner of Seventh and Wabash and welcomed many new visitors to the city. The Naylor Opera House was built at the corner of Fourth and Wabash in 1870. The theater offered a variety of performances until the building was destroyed by fire in 1896. It was later replaced by the Grand Opera House at the corner of Seventh and Cherry in 1897. For those who were not interested in the arts, Terre Haute also offered the Four-Corner Racetrack, built in 1887. The track was known for showcasing some of the country's best trotters and drivers.

The route of the National Road, now U.S. Highway 40, went straight through Terre Haute, bringing further traffic to the city. It intersected with U.S. Highway 41 at Seventh Street and Wabash Avenue, thus earning the city the nickname the "Crossroads of America." Bridges were also built to connect the future site of West Terre Haute to the blossoming city. In the 1900s, corruption became a problem within the city. Certain groups aimed to expose questionable activities occurring at city hall. Federal oversight was even requested to look over city elections. Election interference was rampant with stuffed ballot boxes, counterfeit ballots, bribed officials and blackmail. There were political scandals and even officials in cahoots with the local breweries. In one such instance, local politicians requested that the chief of police and safety board not enforce the standard closing times for local saloons. This was the beginning of the era when Terre Haute was known as "Sin City."

When Prohibition was enacted in the 1920s, Terre Haute's booming distillery empire all but dried up, and work became hard to come by. However, the city of Terre Haute had a trick up its sleeve—a subterranean network of tunnels provided the perfect cover for the bootlegging of liquor. There are still tunnels located beneath much of downtown Terre Haute, though many of them have not been accessed in years and it would be quite dangerous for anyone to attempt to do so. This underground activity invited bank robbers and other criminals to the city, as Terre Haute had gained a reputation as a safe haven for those on the wrong side of the law. John Dillinger frequently visited Terre Haute, and it is said that he stayed at the Terre Haute House. It is also reported that Dillinger once said that he would never rob a bank in the city for fear of being stopped by a train during his escape. It is also believed that Al Capone often visited Terre Haute, engaging in the local brothels and gambling establishments the city had to offer. The new Terre Haute House, built in 1928, continued to serve in the same capacity as the former hotel, allowing Al Capone and other gangsters a place to stay when visiting the city, albeit in a grander setting.

Brothels were a common sight in Terre Haute during this time. Madame Edith Brown owned the premier house of ill repute in the city, the Circle R. Madame Brown kept things classy at her establishment. Her girls were well taken care of, and they were adorned in fine clothing, even having formal nights where the gentleman callers were dressed in tuxedos and an upscale dinner was served. During Prohibition, Madame Brown continued her successful business, acquiring liquor from Kentucky to serve at her brothel. The era of Sin City continued for a number of years before the outbreak of World War II slowed the debauchery. Wartime manufacturers threatened to take their business elsewhere if the city continued to allow prostitution. In response, an ordinance was enacted closing all of the brothels in Terre Haute.

The war actually proved to be good for Terre Haute. The city was not a large manufacturing center for durable goods, so it remained mostly unphased by the conflict. However, this was essentially like putting a band-aid on a wound that needs stitches. In the years following the war, unemployment plagued the city. Factories packed up and left, forcing the city to spend the last few decades struggling to overcome the crisis. In the last few years, Terre Haute has experienced a resurgence. Abandoned factories and store fronts are seeing new life, and tourism is slowly returning to the area. Small businesses are blossoming, and the downtown area is beginning to experience a revitalization. The city has many museums, art galleries, festivals and even a drive-in movie theater. Progress is continuing with further plans for the downtown area and continued expansion on the city's east side.

In this new modern age, Terre Haute seems to be thriving once again with new opportunities on the horizon, leaving the citizens optimistic for a new era in the city's history. However, sometimes progress and renovation can have an unexpected result, namely causing the ghostly inhabitants of a location to take note of the changes as well. One has to wonder if they are already watching the progress, just waiting to reveal themselves to the living residents of Terre Haute.

Happy haunting!

First Spiritualist Society of Terre Haute

Pence Hall—Formerly Located at Second Street and Ohio Street

Following the Civil War, many families were left with feelings of loss and sorrow after the deaths of so many fathers, sons and brothers on the battlefield. These families were searching for some kind of closure. Spiritualism, also known as the "harmonial philosophy," was the belief in communication with the dearly departed, and it was a common practice during the mid- to late 1800s. Spiritualists believe that the spirits of the dead exist and have both the ability and the propensity to communicate with the living. The afterlife, or the "spirit world," is seen by Spiritualists not as a static place but as one in which spirits continue to evolve and change. Many prominent Spiritualists were women and, like most Spiritualists, supported causes such as the abolition of slavery and women's suffrage. Sir Arthur Conan Doyle, the author of stories featuring Sherlock Holmes, was also a known Spiritualist.

Terre Haute was a haven for the Spiritualist movement. Speakers on the subject first visited Terre Haute in 1856. These speakers included Miss Emma Jay, who presented three public lectures to packed audiences. Another notable Spiritualist who visited Terre Haute was Andrew Jackson Davis, also known as the Seer of Poughkeepsie. He and his wife stayed in Terre Haute for several days, and many locals and out-of-town visitors attended the lectures by Mr. Davis. Spiritualism had officially found a home in Terre Haute.

Vintage image of Pence Hall. *Courtesy of the Vigo County Historical Society.*

In May 1867, the First Spiritualist Society of Terre Haute was founded. Dr. Allen Pence, a local doctor and botanic druggist, helped to spearhead, promote and lead the movement. Also instrumental in the creation of the society were contractor and former mayor of Terre Haute James Hook, contractor Tindall A. Madison and Winfield Smith. In September 1867, Dr. Pence donated the second floor of his building, Pence Hall, formerly at the southwest corner of Second and Ohio Streets, to be the society's headquarters. Once the location was selected, all the society needed was a face for the new movement.

In 1873 a new family moved to Terre Haute—Mr. and Mrs. John and Anna Stewart and their children. Though Anna could not read or write, she did possess a unique ability: Anna could speak with the dead. Anna first experienced the ability to communicate with those who had crossed over in 1860. Her otherworldly contacts would sometimes keep John up at night, forcing him to sleep with the lights on in an attempt to fend off the spirits seeking to communicate with Anna. By the time they moved to Terre Haute, Anna had been communicating with spirits for thirteen years, but she had never considered her ability as a means to make money to support her family. When she heard about the First Spiritualist Society of Terre Haute, she was interested in the group and made an "innocent debut" to show off her skills. Anna's first séance so impressed Dr. Pence that he offered Anna and her family free lodging at Pence Hall in exchange for further séances. She accepted the offer and entered into a partnership with the doctor.

Thanks to the efforts of Dr. Pence and Anna, Terre Haute soon become known as a Spiritualism center with people coming from all across the United States to attend lectures and séances at Pence Hall. As a result, Anna was thrust into the national spotlight and became quite well known for her abilities. Each attendee at Pence Hall paid a fifty-cent admission fee, and for those who wanted a more one-on-one opportunity to see Anna work, a private séance could be purchased for five dollars—quite an extravagance in the late 1800s. Sometimes newspapers would enlist reporters in disguise to see if they just might catch Anna in the act of deceit. Some claimed to be successful, but no evidence was ever brought forth to prove the claims of those reporters.

Attendees to Anna's séances would be escorted by a "committee of ladies" who would lead the attendees into a small room lit by gaslight. Once inside, the door was closed and the lights were dimmed, giving some attendees an ominous feeling. Séances require a certain ambiance after all. Dr. Pence would ask the audience for complete silence as Anna attempted to begin her communication with the souls of the dead. As a music box played, it was requested that the patrons direct their attention to a curtain in the room. From behind the curtain, arms and fingers appeared. Other visitors reported seeing the ghostly white face of a man, while still others claimed to see random images materialize from behind the curtain.

As Anna began to hone her abilities, she soon found the ability to communicate with the spirits of famous individuals including George Washington, Andrew Jackson and Abraham Lincoln. This likely increased traffic to Pence Hall, giving visitors the opportunity to speak with the long-deceased early leaders of the United States. President Lincoln's wife, Mary Todd Lincoln, is thought to have been a believer in Spiritualism, which makes sense considering the traumatic way in which her husband's life was taken. It is reported that Mrs. Lincoln had many séances at the White House in an attempt to reach her husband and the spirits of her three children, who passed at young ages. Only one of Lincoln's children, Robert, lived into adulthood.

In December 1882, Anna's abilities were questioned once again when Dr. W. Harry Powell arrived in Terre Haute all the way from Philadelphia. Dr. Powell had traveled to Pence Hall with one goal—to challenge Anna's abilities to communicate with the dead. Dr. Powell was also a medium, and his specialty was the ability to receive written messages from spirits on a slate. He asked Anna to imitate his ability. As mentioned earlier, Anna could not read or write, but Anna was able to replicate Dr. Powell's demonstration, and she took it a step further by using a pencil to inscribe the messages she received from the spirits onto a sheet of paper. One would think that Dr. Powell would have been impressed with Anna's abilities, but instead he flew into a rage, claiming that to test Anna's true abilities, he needed to see her work outside of Pence Hall. Powell believed that by removing her from the location, he would relieve her of any tricks that might be used at Pence Hall, allowing him to out her as a fraud. He even offered to pay her for a demonstration at another site, with local papers reporting on the proposal. By the end of Dr. Powell's confrontation with Anna, Mayor James Hook was forced to diffuse the situation with his fists. Not long after the embarrassing situation with Dr. Powell, Anna ended her marriage with John Stewart. By September 1883, Anna had a new gentleman in her life, and she announced her intention to marry William P. Walling of Battle Creek, Michigan, and retire from her position at Pence Hall. Not much is known about Anna's life following her time at Pence Hall, but it is likely she took a job doing what many disgraced mediums of the day did, spending her time debunking other mediums and exposing them as frauds. As for Dr. Allen Pence, he remained a believer in the "harmonial philosophy" until his

Allen Pence grave at Highland Lawn Cemetery. *Courtesy of Elizabeth Christjansen.*

death on January 22, 1908. He is buried in a small plot at Highland Lawn Cemetery, perhaps waiting for a medium to contact him on the other side.

By 1897 Spiritualism had more than eight million followers in the United States and Europe. However, numbers quickly declined due to the constant attacks of skeptics, including Harry Houdini. Houdini spent a great deal of his life debunking the methods of famous mediums—even going so far as to perform their tricks during his stage shows. Spiritualism also hadn't been a very organized movement, mostly because there was infighting and internal politics among its leaders, which put a strain on the members as well. And with so many mediums being denounced as frauds, it became difficult for the public to trust the abilities of those who claimed to be mediums and even more difficult for true mediums to risk exposing themselves to a public that no longer believed their abilities to be valid.

WOODLAWN CEMETERY

1230 NORTH THIRD STREET, TERRE HAUTE, INDIANA 47807

Woodlawn Cemetery, previously known as City Cemetery, is located on a very crowded section of North Third Street in Terre Haute. The cemetery goes unnoticed by many despite its location. When the cemetery was founded, this would have been the outskirts of town—still densely wooded and not visited by many.

Before delving into the residents and the ghostly activity of Woodlawn Cemetery, it is important to know a bit more about the history of Terre Haute's cemeteries. Terre Haute's first cemetery was located on the Wabash River and is now known as Indian Orchard, most likely due to an account printed in an early newspaper. The cemetery was often referred to as the "Burying Ground" or the "Old Cemetery" in early records, and the first burials are thought to date back to 1816. However, the fictional tale of a Native American brave, Nemo, and his wife, Lena, would forever change the name and history of the burying ground. As the story goes, the two met when Lena was being held captive by Nemo's tribe. Following their marriage, they reportedly returned to the spot near the river that had once been the Wea Indian village called Quiateno (Rising Sun), which is now Terre Haute. Upon arriving, they discovered that the village had been destroyed. Despite the tragedy encountered by the former residents, Nemo and Lena stayed and built a home there. Lena planted apple seeds that grew into a beautiful orchard. They flourished in their new home and were soon blessed with a son. Unfortunately, happiness was not to be for the family, as not long afterward, they were attacked by a marauding group of Miami Indians. Nemo was killed and Lena, fearing for the safety of her newborn son, tossed the child into the arms of one of the attackers, ensuring that he would be adopted into the tribe. Lena then killed herself. It is said that the burying ground was located near the apple orchard. In truth, there had been an orchard, but it was near a Native American settlement in Terre Haute's very early history. Due to this story in the newspaper, people began referring to the burying ground as Indian Orchard. It has even been reported to be an Indian burial ground, but that has also been found to be untrue despite constant circulation of the story over the years. The story of Indian Orchard does not end with the confusion over its name or the origin of the location.

The residents of Indian Orchard Cemetery have been disturbed on a few occasions since beginning their eternal sleep at the beautiful spot overlooking the river. In 1848 the Wabash Erie Canal was the first bit of construction to tear a path through the cemetery. The canal went straight through the center of the two-acre plot, displacing many of the burials. The cemetery had been closed for nine years at this point—since July 3, 1839, just two days after Woodlawn Cemetery opened for burials—so the city had to notify the families of those who would be affected by the canal. The city published notices stating that those affected by the canal would need to be moved to either Woodlawn Cemetery, at that point still being referred to as City Cemetery, or to the east side of Indian Orchard, as that section would not be affected by the canal. It was estimated that fifteen to twenty graves were moved at that time, and arrangements were made for the burials that remained unclaimed. Indian Orchard would be disturbed once again in 1930, when human skulls and skeletons were discovered during excavation to build the foundation for the American Can Company.

The American Can Company site functioned as an industrial property for a number of years before being purchased and converted into luxury lofts that opened in 2018. During renovations at the site in early 2018, workers discovered previously undocumented remains on the property. In January 2018, a human skull was found at the site and was ruled to be from a former burial at Indian Orchard. Then in April 2018, a coffin and human remains were unearthed at the northeast edge of the site. The remains were those of a twenty-something woman who was likely left behind during one of the previous disturbances at the cemetery. A single bone belonging to the remains of six-year-old was also found upon further investigation. It is likely that all three sets of remains belonged to an abandoned row of burials in the cemetery that were either forgotten or ignored because no one claimed them. It will be interesting to see if any former, or possibly current, residents of the Indian Orchard site find their way into the new lofts.

All that remains of Indian Orchard today is a recently added sign retelling the fictional tale of Nemo and Lena and the sad story of Indian Orchard Cemetery. The sign is actually an area of great contention for some locals, as they feel it helps to further circulate the fictional account of Indian Orchard's history. Directly behind the sign is a set of stairs that leads visitors down to the riverfront. The route is littered with trash and graffiti, leaving no sign that part of the cemetery once stood there. Despite the debris, the site is serene with a beautiful view of the Wabash River. One can't help but sense a haunting and sad feeling at the site—as if some of the spirits still remain, and it is quite possible that there are remains left to be unearthed at the site.

Terre Haute's other early cemetery was referred to as the "Public Burial Ground." It was located at the northeast corner of what is now Sixth Street and Ohio Street. Oddly enough, during the 1820s, some graves were moved

The stairs leading to the former site of Indian Orchard Cemetery. *Courtesy of Elizabeth Christjansen.*

Markers of Revolutionary War soldiers formerly at Indian Orchard Cemetery, but who are now buried at Woodlawn Cemetery. *Courtesy of the Vigo County Historical Society.*

from the Public Burial Ground to Indian Orchard, so it is possible that those poor souls had to be moved once again when Indian Orchard was later disturbed. Not much else is known about the Public Burial Ground, but legends have long circulated among Terre Haute's residents, claiming that there could still be burials located at the site and that when one is driving down Ohio Street, you may actually be driving over the graves of some of Terre Haute's earliest settlers. Unfortunately, due to a lack of records, it is impossible to tell whether or not any of Terre Haute's first residents still remain at the site.

As Terre Haute grew, Indian Orchard and the Public Burial Ground soon become far too overcrowded, and it became necessary to open the first City Cemetery, known today as Woodlawn. Thirteen acres were set aside for the cemetery. Brush was cleared and a wooden fence was erected to protect the site. The first interment at Woodlawn was Mary Herrington. She died of scarlet fever, somewhere between four and five years of age, and was buried on July 28, 1839. When walking through Woodlawn Cemetery, any tombstones with dates earlier than that have come from either Indian Orchard or the Public Burial Ground. Eleven names still exist in the records for burials moved from Indian Orchard to Woodlawn, and these interments include three Revolutionary War soldiers.

Many notable Terre Haute residents have been buried at Woodlawn Cemetery. In Division Thirty-Five, you will find the grave of Alice Fischer Harcourt, a stage actress who began her career in Terre Haute before moving to New York City. She gained notoriety for forming the first professional club for women of the theater, called the Twelfth Night Club, which is still in existence to this day. Ed Shouse was a member of John Dillinger's gang, and he is said to be buried in Division Thirty-Seven. Shouse was a trusted member of the Dillinger gang until he flipped on the group, recounting the various robberies that the gang had committed. He even stated that Dillinger had planned to rob the Dixie Flyer train as it passed through Terre Haute. I have taken several trips to Woodlawn Cemetery to find the grave of Ed Shouse, but I have come to the conclusion that he was either buried in an unmarked grave or that his stone has been battered by nature and is no longer legible.

Woodlawn Cemetery is also home to a bit of ghostly activity. There are a handful of mausoleums located in the cemetery, and one stands out. If you drive to the back of the cemetery, you'll find the mausoleum

The front of the Warren mausoleum at Woodlawn Cemetery. *Courtesy of Elizabeth Christjansen.*

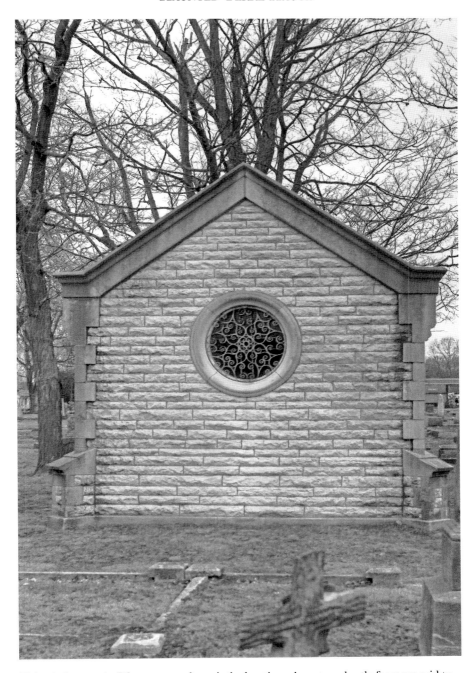

This window on the Warren mausoleum is the location where two ghostly faces are said to appear. *Courtesy of Elizabeth Christjansen.*

of the Warren family. The mausoleum houses the remains of four members of the family. The youngest daughter, Jessie, died on July 30, 1882, at the age of twenty-one. It was reported in the *Saturday Evening Mail* that she died of typhoid fever while visiting the Hotel St. Louis in Lake Minnetonka in Minnesota. Jessie's younger sister, Mary Alice, is also interred in the mausoleum. She outlived Jessie by fifty-five years, passing away at her home in Terre Haute of a cerebral hemorrhage on January 8, 1937. The girls' mother and father are also interred within the family mausoleum. The story of their parents is a sad one. Their mother, Martha Ellen Clark Warren, died at the age of thirty-five, little more than a year after giving birth to Mary Alice. Their father, Levi G. Warren, was a local businessman and was elected president of the First National Bank of Terre Haute. However, death struck the family once more when Levi died of a sudden illness at the age of forty-nine on June 29, 1865, leaving the girls as orphans. Fortunately, Martha and Levi had an older daughter, Sallie, who, along with her husband, took the girls in and raised them as their own.

In the years since, the Warren mausoleum has reportedly become quite the hot spot for ghostly activity. Most of the stories focus on the ornate window at the back of the mausoleum. Many visitors to the cemetery claim to have witnessed two faces staring back at them through the window. They describe the faces as being that of a man with thick sideburns, who is in his late thirties or early forties, and a young woman with light hair tied into a bun, who is in her twenties. Shadows have also been reported moving around near the Warren mausoleum, but these tales are far less frequent than the accounts of ghostly faces in the window. Could these be the spirits of Levi Warren and his young daughter Jessie? Or perhaps the woman is Martha Ellen, reuniting with her husband in the afterlife after losing one another so young.

Spirit orbs, which are thought to be the energy of spirits or entities manifesting themselves as a glowing ball of light, have also been seen and photographed in several locations within the cemetery. These orbs are thought to contain the energy of one or more spirits and can be seen and photographed in a variety of colors. For those looking to visit Woodlawn Cemetery, please keep in mind that the cemetery closes at dusk and trespassing after dark is not appreciated.

HIGHLAND LAWN CEMETERY

4420 WABASH AVENUE.
TERRE HAUTE. INDIANA 47803

Highland Lawn Cemetery would become Terre Haute's fourth cemetery. The location was chosen because of its beauty but also because it was known as a peaceful spot situated on high rolling hills on the outskirts of the city. Initially there was some opposition to the location. Some were concerned it would be unfit for a burial ground—that it was too wet and marshy, which would possibly cause issues with burials. The land had previously been a farm and served as an early distillery. Despite concerns, the cemetery opened its gates in 1884. The entrance includes a Romanesque Revival bell tower constructed of limestone from Bedford, Indiana. The Gothic-style arch that greets visitors upon arriving at Highland Lawn was designed by Paul Leizt of Chicago and constructed by Edward Hazledine. The cemetery's chapel, built nine years after the cemetery opened, is also of the Romanesque style. It is located on the highest hill in the cemetery. The chapel features gabled roofs, a domed brick basement and stained-glass windows. The first burial at Highland Lawn was Samantha McPherson, who died at age thirty on October 13, 1884, of typhoid fever. She was buried in section two, lot six on October 29, 1884. Highland Lawn is the second-largest cemetery in Indiana and is home to some ornate and stunning tombstones, mausoleums and sculptures. The cemetery was added to the National Register of Historic Places on November 29, 1990.

The cemetery is also the final resting place of some of Terre Haute's most notable residents. Eugene V. Debs, a well-known union leader,

Vintage image of the arch and bell tower at Highland Lawn Cemetery. *Courtesy of the Vigo County Historical Society.*

Socialist and activist, is buried in section 3. Debs ran for president of the United States on several occasions and was a constant fixture in Terre Haute in his final years. He died of heart failure at the age of seventy on October 20, 1926. Max Erhmann was a Terre Haute attorney and writer of the poem "Desiderata." Erhmann gained fame when many of his poems were published after his death. His family once maintained a garment business at the corner of Ninth and Wabash, with Max running his law practice from the location. Many said he participated in very little legal work, instead choosing to focus his time on his writing. The Ehrmann monument is fairly easy to recognize as it is a sculpture of a large angel standing in front of a cross. Hollywood vamp and vaudeville actress Valeska Suratt is buried in section 14, lot 475.5. Suratt starred in several successful silent movies before returning to vaudeville, performing well into the 1920s.

Highland Lawn was also the location of a brutal murder, but the acts that followed may be more disturbing than the crime itself. On February

25, 1901, Ida Finkelstein, a local school teacher, had ridden the interurban out to the stop that once served Highland Lawn Cemetery. The former station now functions as the cemetery office. Ida had been staying with a family nearby, but before she could make it to her destination, tragedy struck. Ida would later be found on the front porch of a home near the cemetery. Her throat had been slashed, and she had suffered a gunshot wound to the back. She was rushed to Union Hospital with part of the blade still in her neck. Ida did not survive her wounds, but before she passed away, she was able to give the police a name. She believed her assailant to be a local African American man named George Ward. She claimed that he had robbed her of five dollars before inflicting the vicious wounds. Ward was identified as having been at the interurban stop that day and as the owner of a knife that was missing a blade. He was immediately apprehended by police.

Authorities at the time claimed Ward confessed to the crime. Though in the years since, that confession has come into question. The police were looking to punish someone, and George Ward was the easy suspect. Some wonder if his confession was made under duress, or perhaps out of fear of

Chapel at Highland Lawn Cemetery. *Courtesy of Elizabeth Christjansen.*

retaliation from officers, he confessed to protect himself. It is also possible that George Ward committed the murder of Ida Finkelstein. Sadly, we will never know.

Following Ward's arrival at the local jail, a crowd of angry citizens formed outside. Police Superintendent Charles E. Hyland made the decision to wire the governor of Indiana to request assistance. The National Guard in Terre Haute was placed on alert, and plans were made to move Ward to Indianapolis. The mob continued to grow, reaching nearly one thousand people in a short time. Before the superintendent could have Ward removed from the building, angry citizens began to attack the side door of the jail, using a twenty-five-foot-by-eight-foot timber as a battering ram. When they breeched the door, people flooded into the jail. The jailers were overwhelmed, and George Ward was forcibly removed from the jail. He cried for help, but his pleas were silenced by a blow from a sledge hammer. It is possible that George Ward died at that moment, but the mob didn't care—they wanted violent justice. What occurred next would leave a dark stain on the history of Terre Haute.

A noose was crafted from horse halters and tightened around George's neck. His limp body was taken to the old Wabash River drawbridge, where the noose was attached to a chain that dangled from the bridge. George Ward's body was then tossed over the railing and left to hang lifelessly for all in the massive mob to view. Apparently, the act of committing Terre Haute's first and only lynching was not enough for the crowd. Their blood lust could not be quenched, so when someone suggested that George's body be burned, no one intervened. Turpentine and wood were acquired in short order and a pyre was created on the river bank. The rope was then cut, sending George's body into the flames. By this point, more than two thousand people had gathered at the site, some of whom cheered when George's body landed in the fire. However, the worst was yet to come. Once the fire was extinguished, onlookers helped themselves to souvenirs, taking pieces of George's clothing, shoes and even bits of his bones—essentially reveling in the heinous act. George never received a proper burial, and one has to wonder if his spirit remains at the site of his grisly slaying. On the day following George's murder, members of the Terre Haute community attended a funeral for Ida Finkelstein. She was later interred at Highland Lawn Cemetery in section 21E, lot 22. She was twenty-one years old.

Highland Lawn Cemetery has gained a reputation as the most haunted location in Terre Haute. The remains of Claude Herbert, the hero of one of Terre Haute's most tragic stories, are interred in a mausoleum located just off of the main driveway as you head into the cemetery. On the evening of December 19, 1898, on the northeast corner of Wabash Avenue and Fifth Street in downtown Terre Haute, Claude Herbert was playing Santa Claus at the Havens and Geddes Department Store. At the time, the store took up the entire block and was the largest in Indiana. Claude had been hired two days earlier, having just arrived home from duty during the Spanish-American War. Claude had been in dire need of a job to support his newly widowed mother, Mattie, so he took the position as Santa.

While he was working as Santa in the basement, an incandescent light bulb popped in a display window, setting the items around it on fire. With the fire spreading quickly, another employee notified Claude of the situation. At the time, he was surrounded by nearly thirty young children and no doubt concerned for their well-being. Despite the dire situation, Claude kept a cool head, opting to stay in character as Santa to calm the children as he shuffled them outside to safety. Upon exiting the building, Claude was alerted to the fact that there could still be victims trapped in the inferno. Rather than allow the responding firefighters to clear the building, Claude's military training went into effect. He threw his Santa costume to the ground and reentered the building. Onlookers last saw him take a deep breath before he disappeared into the thick smoke once again.

As Claude was a newly hired employee, he was unfamiliar with the layout of the large department store and was unaware of a tunnel that led from the basement to a warehouse on Cherry Street. The employees that Claude so desperately searched for had escaped through that underground exit. Claude, likely disoriented from the smoke, was unable to find the same exit. Witnesses claim that Claude was last seen trying to save himself from the fire. Some said he jumped from a second-floor window, but others reported seeing him jump from the fifth floor. This seems to be the mostly likely scenario, as that is where he had dressed to play Santa earlier in the evening and he would have been familiar with that location. Claude Herbert was not the only hero to lose his life that day. Firefighter John Osterloo died, and Henry Nehf, a volunteer firefighter, also perished in a nearby building. The final victim of the fire was store clerk Katie Maloney. She was trapped by the blaze and jumped from a second-story ledge. Upon impact, she hit her head and sustained fatal injuries. Three days later, amid the smoldering ruins of the Havens and Geddes Department Store, estimated to be nearly $2 million in property damage, searchers found one of Herbert's bones. The location led investigators to believe that Claude must have been on the fifth floor when he jumped. No further remains were discovered. Claude Herbert had been entirely cremated by the blaze. His remains are interred at the mausoleum at Highland Lawn Cemetery.

In the years since Claude's heroic sacrifice, there has been strange activity reported near the tomb. Visitors who have taken photographs of the area report catching orbs in some of their photographs, with the balls of light centered directly on the Herbert family plot. Whether this is the spirit of Claude Herbert or just a trick of light, it is nice to think that the spirit of Terre Haute's hero may still be looking out for the citizens of the city.

Not far from the Herbert mausoleum, a trio of red tombstones in section 14, lot 198 reveals the story of a ghastly triple homicide that occurred near West Terre Haute on May 4, 1914. Roughly thirty gypsies had traveled from Kentucky to Terre Haute, arriving on May 1, 1914. They parked their wagons near Paris Road and set up a camp. On the day before the homicides, members of the gypsy caravan were in high spirits—they were in the middle of a raucous celebration, consuming eight kegs of beer, wine and ale in the process. The celebration lasted into the wee hours of the morning, following which most of the gypsies either went to sleep or passed out from the alcohol. But one man remained awake.

John Demetro was a Brazilian gypsy tribal chief traveling with the caravan. On the morning of May 4, John was probably quite inebriated. He was troubled by rumors circulating throughout the encampment that his common law wife, Socca Riska, was having an affair. He also believed that Socca's father, Bob, and brother, Joe, were keeping her secret. At some point, John entered the tent where his family slept. He brutally bludgeoned and shot Socca before turning the gun on his in-laws. The gypsies in the camp, alarmed by the gunfire, ran to the Riska tent. They found that Socca and Bob had died instantly from their injuries, but Joe, who had been shot in the face, was still alive despite the fact that he was missing a large portion of his head. John Demetro, however, could not be found. Some of the gypsies rushed to a nearby saloon, while others headed to a local farmhouse to alert the authorities of the murders. The West Terre Haute police arrived quickly and were no doubt shocked by the scene before them. Joe Riska was rushed to a local hospital, but sadly, due to the severity of his injuries, he died the following day. The gypsies warned police that John Demetro would likely be accompanied by his sixteen-shot

Remington rifle. The police, prepared for a shootout with Demetro, found him sitting near his tent, his rifle across his lap. The man stared blankly at the ground, likely already haunted by the murders he had committed. Demetro did not resist arrest but calmly passed his rifle to the police before he was taken into custody without incident.

Following the murders, the caravan moved east of Terre Haute and began preparations for the Riska funeral. The gypsies purchased extravagant caskets for the family. They also visited the upscale shops of Terre Haute, purchasing the finest attire for the Riskas. When the day of the funeral came, mourning gypsies from throughout the Midwest were in attendance. Incense balls were burned during the graveside service, with pipes and tobacco placed next to each of the bodies. Following the lowering of the coffins, the mourners sprinkled them with soil. Bottles of wine were broken, and wine was poured on the coffins in the shape of a cross. According to witnesses, the funeral was a sight to behold.

Demetro was arraigned on May 8, 1914. He argued that he was acting in self-defense, but evidence suggested otherwise. He was charged with murder, and a trial would commence in September 1914. The trial

The Riska graves at Highland Lawn Cemetery. Reports of the supernatural have long been associated with this trio of graves. *Courtesy of Elizabeth Christjansen.*

would be postponed on two occasions and was later scheduled to begin in September 1915. The trial was attended by many of the gypsies who had been present at the camp when the Riska murders occurred. By the end of the day, they would find themselves disappointed with the outcome of the trial. Demetro's defense argued that he would not receive a fair trial in Terre Haute due to the attention the case had received. The judge agreed, and it was decided that the trial would be moved to Rockville, Indiana. Following the change of venue and one more continuance, the prosecutor and Demetro's defense attorney negotiated a plea agreement. The charges for the deaths of Bob Riska and his son were dropped with Demetro agreeing to plead guilty to second-degree murder for the death of Socca. He was sentenced to life and ordered to serve his time at the Indiana State Prison in Michigan City. Almost two years after the murders, Demetro had become a shell of his former self. He had lost a considerable amount of weight, and his incarceration had taken a toll on his mental health. He spent the majority of his time in the infirmary while in prison, costing the facility a pretty penny in medical care. Interestingly, after only eighteen months in prison, Demetro was paroled—likely due to his deteriorating health and the estimated cost of his continued care. He was deported to Brazil, where he later died.

Though the murders took place 105 years ago, the gypsy community still mourns the loss of the Riska family. In the years since, descendants of the gypsy caravan have been seen visiting the graves in Highland Lawn Cemetery. Perhaps they are performing rituals to honor the dead or ensuring that the spirits of the Riska family remain peacefully at rest. Despite the rituals, otherworldly occurrences have been reported in the area around the Riska graves.

Rumors have circulated about gypsy ghosts walking among the tombstones. Could these be the spirits of the Riska family eternally drawn to the site of their burials? Or perhaps they are looking for the caravan they lost so long ago. Orbs have been seen floating above the family plot, usually in multiples. This has led some to believe that these could be manifestations of the Riska family. Visitors to the graves have also noted feeling an extreme sense of sadness and grief. The rituals performed by the gypsies could account for some of the melancholy felt at the site—almost as if their sorrow has left a permanent mark in the area surrounding the Riska plot. While it is possible that these strange occurrences stem from the gypsies' belief in the supernatural world, it is also possible that the Riska family is unable to rest following such sudden and violent deaths.

Regardless, the trio of graves remains one of the most visited locations within the cemetery.

Though the Riska graves may be a frequented site in the cemetery, they are far from the most well known. My mother never missed an opportunity to tell me about her ghostly encounter at Highland Lawn Cemetery. Sometime in the 1970s, she and three friends ventured into Highland Lawn after dark. I would imagine that such an act was frowned upon then, and just a reminder, it is still frowned upon now, so please do not try to enter the cemetery after dark. The two boys in the cemetery with my mother thought they would play a prank, leaving my mother and her friend stranded and alone in the cemetery. Though the boys were only gone for fifteen minutes, my mother said it felt like an eternity, especially since she and her friend kept hearing a little dog bark and the calming voice of a man, though they could not see them.

This brings us to the most well-known haunt of Highland Lawn: a little bulldog named Stiffy Green. As most Terre Haute locals know, Stiffy Green was the pet bulldog and beloved companion of local florist John G. Heinl. The dog is described as having a stiff gait and beautiful emerald green eyes, hence the name Stiffy Green. John Heinl originally arrived in Terre Haute in 1863, quickly establishing a thriving floral business. He also met his future wife, Mary Debs, the older sister of Eugene V. Debs, and together they had two sons, Fred and Robert. When he wasn't supplying flowers to the community of Terre Haute, Heinl spent his time working with local organizations and businesses, such as the Rose Dispensary and the Rose Orphans Home. He was known to be quite a charitable gentleman and was liked by the citizens of Terre Haute. Despite Heinl's busy schedule, he was always accompanied by his bulldog, and Stiffy Green was reported to have been a constant sight at Heinl's floral shop at 129 South Seventh Street. Some reports claim that the dog was not very friendly, preferring to spend his time at John's side, though he did take to the occasional customer.

John Heinl died at his residence on December 30, 1920, at the age of seventy-six. Following the funeral, his body was taken to his mausoleum in Highland Lawn Cemetery. We have all heard stories about the sadness that a pet can experience upon losing their owner, and little Stiffy Green was no different. He would travel to the mausoleum every day, only to be found later by the Heinl family, mournfully waiting on the mausoleum steps for his master. Finally, the family decided to let Stiffy Green reside at the cemetery full-time with cemetery staff tending to

The mausoleum of John G. Heinl at Highland Lawn Cemetery. Stiffy Green once made his home inside this tomb. *Courtesy of Elizabeth Christjansen.*

his needs and ensuring that he had food. One day, the cemetery staff contacted the family to notify them that Stiffy Green had passed away on the mausoleum steps, most surely of a broken heart. It seemed fitting to them to have the little bulldog stuffed, compete with a set of emerald glass eyes, so he could spend eternity with the master he was so devoted to in life. Stiffy Green was placed in the back of the mausoleum and could only to be viewed through the ornate mausoleum door. It wasn't long before stories began to circulate that if you went to Highland Lawn Cemetery at night, you would hear the voice of a man and his small dog roaming the cemetery. They have sometimes been seen but are often only heard in the distance.

The story doesn't end there. Stiffy Green resided in the mausoleum with his master for several years. It became a favorite spot for local teenagers, like my mother, who would go there to shine flashlights into the mausoleum and hope to be greeted by the specters of John G. Heinl and his little green-eyed bulldog. However, sometime in the 1980s, vandals entered the cemetery with ill intent toward the bulldog, and they shot a gun into the Heinl Mausoleum, shattering one of Stiffy Green's

Stiffy Green, with his bags and photo of John Heinl, ready to move to the new museum. *Courtesy of the Vigo County Historical Society.*

eyes. In 1989 it was decided that Stiffy Green should be moved to the Vigo County Historical Society, now located at 929 Wabash Avenue in Terre Haute. He can be found safely residing there today, guarding a small replica of the Heinl mausoleum. But is the tale of Stiffy Green really what it appears to be?

Through the years, I have heard multiple accounts stating that the little dog wasn't really a dog at all, but a statue. The most well-known story seems to be that Stiffy Green was nothing more than a favorite lawn ornament of John Heinl. After he passed away, the family thought it fitting to place the statue in the mausoleum as a tribute to Heinl. However, there are still many locals who disagree with this claim.

My stepfather once told me a different story. During a brief tenure working at a local monument company in the 1970s, a coworker told him that Stiffy Green had indeed been the faithful companion of John Heinl. Following Stiffy Green's death, he was stuffed and put in the mausoleum as the legend states, but not long afterward, the little dog was stolen from the Heinl mausoleum, prompting the family to replace him with a concrete statue—the same statue that now resides in the Vigo County Historical Society. My mother also strongly believed that Stiffy Green had been a real dog, but perhaps, instead of being stuffed and placed in the mausoleum after John Heinl's death, the family placed a concrete statue in honor of the bond that Heinl and Stiffy Green shared in life. Many locals will agree that there may be some truth to the existence of the little bulldog and his master and their eternal evening strolls through Highland Lawn Cemetery.

As you wind your way out of the cemetery, there is another mausoleum—this one belonging to the Sheets family. Martin Alonzo Sheets was a local Terre Haute stockbroker who became a successful cattle farmer after retirement. Like many others during the early twentieth century, one thing concerned Mr. Sheets greatly. He was petrified of being buried alive, also called taphophobia. He had amassed quite a bit of wealth, and he came up with a rather modern plan to address his concerns regarding premature burial. First, he would have a coffin specially designed with inner latches for escape from the inside. Second, he would have a mausoleum built to avoid being trapped underground. Lastly, and most importantly, he had a phone installed in the mausoleum, so in the event that he woke up inside his coffin, he would be able to call for assistance. It has been said by many that Sheets had the phone connected directly to the cemetery office, so in the event

The Sheets mausoleum at Highland Lawn Cemetery. *Courtesy of Elizabeth Christjansen.*

of his call, they would only need to run mere yards from the office to his mausoleum. Martin Sheets passed away in February 1926. At his request, his body was not embalmed. Sheets was concerned that should he slip into a coma, the act of embalming or undergoing an autopsy would certainly kill him. His mausoleum phone remained connected for a time following his death at the age of seventy-nine, but no calls were ever placed to the cemetery office, and the phone line was eventually disconnected.

Sheets's wife, Susan, lived another three years following her husband's death in 1926. She had been injured in an auto accident in the spring of 1929 and had been living at a home in Paris, Illinois. By all accounts, she had done fairly well following Martin's death, but this is where an otherwise odd story about the fear of premature death takes an even more unusual turn. Upon Mrs. Sheets's death on May 3, 1929, she was found to be tightly clutching the telephone receiver in her hand. The family just assumed she had died while attempting to contact paramedics for assistance. Following a medical exam, it was discovered that Mrs. Sheets had died from a massive heart attack. Doctors assumed that the stress of the car accident may have taken a toll of her heart. Plans were made to have Mrs. Sheets interred in the mausoleum along with her husband, and cemetery workers were dispatched to ready the location. Upon entering the mausoleum, one thing was immediately obvious to the workers: the phone that had been quiet for three long years was now off the hook, as if one final ghostly call had been placed to Mrs. Sheets, perhaps calling her to join her husband on the other side.

Indiana State University

200 North Seventh Street,
Terre Haute, Indiana 47809

Terre Haute is home to four colleges and universities. Two of these institutions of higher learning are known not only for their academics but also for the spirits that reside on campus. Indiana State University (ISU) is located in downtown Terre Haute. The university has humble beginnings and was first known as the Indiana Normal School and later the Indiana State Teacher's College. The creation of the Indiana Normal School began in 1865 when the Indiana state legislature enacted a plan to open a school specializing in the education of teachers. The state offered $50,000 for its part in the plan, but it required a location for this new school and no less than $50,000 in additional money before work on the school could commence. The Board of the Normal School gained approval to advertise throughout the state, hoping to find a city that would meet the criteria. Terre Haute was the only city in the state to offer both funds and land for the project.

On January 6, 1870, the first incarnation of the school opened. It was located on the grounds of the present-day Lincoln Quadrangle or "Quad." The building was only partially finished, but twenty-three students and three assistants were welcomed as the first attendees and employees of the Normal School. The student body would increase to forty later in the year, requiring the school to hire three additional faculty members. The school would operate for eighteen years, welcoming many future teachers through its doors. However, tragedy struck on April 8, 1888, when the building was destroyed by fire. Terre Haute rallied around the displaced students, providing temporary housing and another $50,000 for a new building. Students were welcomed back for classes in the new building in the fall of 1888. A plaque has since been erected in honor of that first building. The stone plaque has an error though—an apostrophe is added to the word *its*. Some students believe that by touching the error, they will be guaranteed good luck on their next test. The school spent these years focused on educating future teachers, so it seems interesting that one of the well-known myths involves a grammatical error.

The Indiana Teacher's College soon began to expand beyond teaching. The college changed names again in 1961 and became known as the Indiana State College, and in 1965 it became Indiana State University. Sadly, only one building, Normal Hall, still stands from the early days of the Indiana Normal School. It was originally constructed in 1910 to serve as a library. The building included an opulent reading room with a dome, which consisted of stained-glass windows that depicted figures famous for their contributions to the arts and philosophy. Normal Hall continued in that capacity until the construction of ISU's current library, Cunningham Memorial Library, in 1974. Following its closure, Normal Hall fell into disrepair. The dome was covered by a drop ceiling, and many of the stained-glass panels, broken after years of neglect, were stored in an attic. The remaining intact panels were displayed in the Cunningham Memorial Library. Fortunately, in 2015 Normal Hall was fully renovated and has reclaimed its early days of grandeur. The stained-glass panels have been re-created, and twenty columns in the reading room were fully restored with a scagliola finish. Though Normal Hall is the only remaining building from the early days of the Normal School, it is most certainly not the only building on campus to have been renovated or changed in some way over time.

I was a student at ISU from 2002 until 2006, so I became familiar with the ghostly legends that circulate on campus. The most well-known ghost of ISU resides in Burford Hall. The six-story residence hall opened on September 13, 1959. The building was originally a dormitory for female students and included communal restrooms on each floor and a lounge for the three hundred students who lived in the building.

As the story goes, Barb was a freshman living in Burford Hall. The dormitory would have been a woman's dorm during the time of Barb's story, but in the years since, the building has become a coed dormitory. After an evening of drinking, Barb returned to the fourth floor of the dorm drunk and very ill. She ventured to the bathroom alone, spending the wee hours of the morning vomiting and crying on the floor. Though

Burford Hall at Indiana State University. The ghosts of Barfing Barb and Charlotte Burford are found here. *Courtesy of Elizabeth Christjansen.*

other students heard Barb, they most likely assumed that she was just ill and would feel better in the morning. At some point the vomiting stopped. When students prepared for class the next morning, no one saw Barb. Sadly, she was found dead on the floor of the bathroom, having succumbed to the effects of alcohol poisoning.

It wasn't long after Barb's death that people began reporting strange occurrences on the fourth floor of Burford Hall. It is likely that dying in such a traumatic way has left Barb's ghost confused, and it is possible that she may not even know she died. Students sometimes hear what sounds like a replaying of Barb's death. They will hear crying from the women's bathroom followed by violent vomiting and the flushing of the toilet, but when they go to check on their peer, no one is in the bathroom. Barb has also been known to haunt the hallways of the fourth floor. She can often be heard laughing, and sometimes students even hear her scream. Strange stains have also been known to appear in the hallway. Some students reported that Barb behaved more like a poltergeist, moving their belongings, turning off alarm clocks and unlocking doors.

A friend of mine lived in Burford Hall while attending ISU, and he reports that though the communal woman's bathroom where Barb would have passed away has been removed, strange things did occur in that area, and students often found themselves baffled by strange happenings in the building. I could find no record of a student dying in such a manner in Burford Hall, but one thing is for certain: whether or not Barb existed, she serves as an excellent cautionary tale for students imbibing at the many bars Terre Haute has to offer.

Barb is not the only ghost rumored to haunt Burford Hall. She is joined by "Old Lady Charlotte Burford," a former dean of female students. Burford served as faculty at ISU for forty-four years—thirty-six of those years as the dean—and is the namesake of Burford Hall. The legend states that Old Lady Burford committed suicide in room 217, and since then, there have been many suicide attempts in her former residence. However, I could find no record of any suicide attempts by students in that room. As it turns out, Charlotte Burford lived to the ripe old age of ninety-one, passing away of natural causes on July 6, 1970, in a nursing facility in Marshall, Illinois. That does not mean that she isn't making her presence known to the students of Burford Hall. Students living in the residence hall report that a painting of Burford seems to follow them as they pass by it. Other reports include strange sounds and the feeling of being watched, even when away from the painting of Charlotte Burford. Perhaps the ghost of Charlotte Burford is just returning to the place she knew best in the afterlife—possibly to ensure that no shenanigans occur in the coed residence hall. Regardless, any ghostly activity that occurs in Burford Hall, aside from Barb's activities on the fourth floor, can often be attributed to Old Lady Burford.

Cromwell Hall is another dormitory on the ISU campus and one of the four buildings in what is known as the Sycamore Tower plaza. Cromwell Hall has a strange story to tell, but the story you get often depends on who you ask. One version states that sometime in the 1990s, a male student was living in room 1221, on the west side of the building. As any student knows, finals can be terribly stressful, and they were for this student. Stressed and not knowing what to do, it is said the student painted a white cross beneath his window before jumping to his death. The cross is said to remain to this day, though many attempts have been made to remove it.

The second version of the story involves a female student who was reported to have fallen from her twelfth-story window, landing on the ground below. Another version of the story involving the female student claims that she used a bedsheet to hang herself from her twelfth-story window. Either way, following her death, the same white cross is said to

Front view of Cromwell Hall at Indiana State University. *Courtesy of Elizabeth Christjansen.*

The side view of Cromwell Hall. The cross is reported to be under the twelfth-floor window on the left. *Courtesy of Elizabeth Christjansen.*

have appeared beneath the window, causing some to believe her death may have occurred under suspicious circumstances. Strange sounds that seem to have no source have also been reported on the twelfth floor of Cromwell Hall. Those who have seen the cross claim that it is large enough to be seen when driving or walking beneath the building. The cross is currently not visible, but many people claim that the brick underneath the window looks as though it has been disturbed—perhaps the result of one of the many attempts to cover the Cromwell Hall Cross.

As a student at ISU, I spent quite a bit of time in Dreiser Hall, and not just because it has its own ghost story to tell. Dreiser was built in 1950, and reports of the building's ghost have circulated for several years and are well known among students. The building is the current home of the ISU student media department, and it houses the old ISU theater, which is rumored to be haunted by a former stage lighting student.

It is thought that the woman died while in school and was unable to finish her degree at ISU. The ghost, lovingly referred to as Karen, is known to cause the lights in the theater to flicker. It is also said that she will correct lighting mistakes made by students, and students in the lighting booth sometimes feel a cold presence on their backs, almost as if someone is leaning over them, ensuring that they make their lighting cues.

Dreiser Hall at Indiana State University is the eternal home of a ghost called Karen. *Courtesy of Elizabeth Christjansen.*

I was recently invited to Dreiser to discuss the ghosts of ISU during a segment for Sycamore Video. As I was speaking about Karen and stating that she was more than welcome to join us for the taping, a student at the back of the room, coincidently also named Karen, felt a cold shiver shoot up her back. This is not the first time that strange activity has occurred when the ghost of Karen is being discussed. During one of my haunted history walking tours, I was standing just underneath the awning at the north entrance of Dreiser Hall. As I told the group the story of Karen, it felt as though someone flicked water on my face. I immediately looked up, but since we hadn't experienced any rain around that time, I was unable to find a concrete cause for the activity. Though the story of Karen does not speculate on what caused her untimely death, there is one aspect that many can agree on: Karen still has a penchant for adjusting the lights.

One of the busiest locations on campus is the Hulman Memorial Student Union. Many students pass through those doors daily—some on their way to Jones Hall, which is located directly behind the Student Union. Jones Hall was built in 1966 to serve as a residence hall, and it still serves in that capacity today. The building was dedicated on January 5, 1967. It was named in honor of William Allen Jones, the first president of the Indiana State Normal School.

Jones Hall is known for having its share of odd activity, but the occurrences at Jones Hall are far less frequent and not as well known as those that occur elsewhere on campus. There was one death in the building that could be attributed to the existence of a male disembodied voice that has been heard by students living and/or visiting the residence hall. On the morning of March 20, 1991, twenty-three-year-old Indiana State student Michael John Deliduka and three of his friends were engaging in an activity called "elevator surfing." Deliduka had used a coat hanger to interrupt the safety mechanism, allowing the doors of the elevator to open despite the fact that the elevator was not yet on the eighth floor where the boys lived. Once the doors were open, Deliduka and his friends had access to both of the building's elevators. As they were riding on top of one of the elevators, the other elevator got stuck. Deliduka moved from the working elevator to the one that had gotten stuck, and as he did so, the elevator engaged, pinning him between the elevator carriage and the shaft wall. Deliduka died instantly, and his cause of death was listed as positional asphyxia.

In the years since his death, the story of Michael John Deliduka has become a cautionary tale that students, especially those living in Jones

Jones Hall at Indiana State University. Ghostly activity has occurred in this residence hall. *Courtesy of Elizabeth Christjansen.*

Hall, are aware of. However, is it possible that his spirit has remained at Jones Hall? Given the fact that he died so quickly, it is possible that, much like the spirit of Barb, he is unaware of his passing and remains in the place that he last remembers. Regardless, it seems that Jones Hall is the home of a male spirit. Though I could find no reports of anyone seeing a ghost—or, really, seeing anything for that matter—students have heard a male voice in Jones Hall. One account from a former student states that she heard a voice while she waited by herself in a friend's dorm room in Jones Hall. Her friend was showering, and they were planning to head to a campus activity, so she was sure that it was not a trick. The voice whispered, "Get out," and she did. After that, she would only return when her friend was in the dorm room. Upon first hearing the story, one might think that "get out" is an ominous phrase to hear from a ghost, but when you consider how Mr. Deliduka died, it is possible that the ghost was referring to being stuck between the elevator carriage and the shaft and that he couldn't get out.

While walking around the campus of Indiana State University, one might be shocked to stumble across a grand home dating back to the 1860s. This residence has historically served as office space for the university as well as the home of some of ISU's presidents. It continues in that capacity to this day and is currently a private residence. However, the home was not always associated with the university. The Condit House was built as a private home in 1860, five years prior to the establishment of the Indiana State Normal School. The house is a fine example of Italianate architecture and is made of brick with a large pavilion sandwiched between two wooden porches. A balcony adorned with iron filigree hangs over the entrance, allowing the home to maintain its original air of sophistication. The residence was built by Lucien Houriet, but he only maintained ownership for three years before selling it in 1863 to Reverend Blackford Condit, the namesake of the Condit House.

Reverend Condit arrived in Terre Haute with his family when he was still a young child. He graduated from Wabash College in 1854 and entered the Lane Theological Seminary, earning his license to be a Presbyterian minister in 1857. After receiving his license, Condit continued his studies and served as a pastor in Ohio, New York and Pennsylvania. After marrying his wife, Sarah Louisa Mills Condit, the reverend returned to Terre Haute and accepted a position as the pastor of the Baldwin Street Presbyterian Church. He would serve in that capacity until 1875. Sarah was the daughter of Caleb Mills, a man considered by many to be the "father of the Indiana public school system." He served as the Second Indiana Superintendent of Public Instruction and as a professor at Wabash College. Sarah's father, along with many other educational leaders throughout the state, often visited the Condit House.

Sarah and Reverend Condit had been married for about a year when they moved into the house with their newborn twins, Charlotte and Charles, who were born on November 23, 1862. It should have been a happy time for the family, but that was not to be. Charlotte passed away when she was three months old, on March 9, 1863, with her brother following her to the spirit realm only six months later on September 1, 1893. I could find no record of what caused the deaths of the Condit children, though it is likely they succumbed to one of the many infectious diseases that were prevalent at the time such as influenza, pneumonia or tuberculosis. Or perhaps, since they were twins, there had been complications at birth that troubled them throughout their short lives. Despite the loss of their twins, the Condits went on to have six more children.

They welcomed their third child, a daughter named Sarah Louisa, on March 26, 1864. Sarah was followed by her sister, Emma, on June 30, 1965. Emma would only live to be twenty-five years year old, as she contracted acute tuberculosis and passed away from the disease on January 31, 1881. The Condits' fifth child was a son, Howe Allen, born on October 4, 1868. The couple's excitement over Howe's birth was cut short when young Sara died only sixteen days later. I could not find any record of what caused Sarah's death, but as with Charlotte and Charles, it is likely that Sarah was the victim of some sort of infectious disease. The Condits named their sixth child Blackford Mills in honor of both his father and grandfather. Blackford was born on December 9, 1871, but as with many of his siblings before him, his life ended at an early age. When Blackford was only twenty, he was stricken with perityphlitis—an inflammation of the connective tissue around the cecum and appendix— and died from the illness on June 1, 1892. The couple welcomed another daughter, Helen, on February 28, 1874, followed by their last child, Joseph Dayton, on April 23, 1877. Joseph studied at the College of Physicians and Surgeons in New York and received his medical degree in 1901. He later opened a private practice in Pasadena, California, in 1904. He remained in Pasadena with his wife, Katherine, until his death on July 5, 1940.

Helen must have been particularly close with her parents, as she lived in the home with them until their deaths. Reverend Condit had fallen into ill health in the years after his retirement, though he continued to serve as a trustee at Wabash College until 1896 and authored several religious texts. Condit passed away on March 27, 1903, and Sarah joined him in eternal rest on March 13, 1914. Following the death of her mother, Helen maintained ownership of the home. She was known to be a kind woman with an interest in seeing Terre Haute prosper. She was also very charitable, contributing to both the Vigo County Historical Society and the Sheldon Swope Art Gallery. Helen's older brother Howe Allen joined her in the home after the loss of their parents. Howe was a well-known attorney in Terre Haute, practicing law in the city for nearly forty years. The siblings lived in the home together until tragedy once again struck the Condit family. On February 17, 1938, Howe was cleaning a gun at the Condit House, just as he had done many times before. Unfortunately, in this instance, the pistol accidently discharged, striking and killing him. Despite her grief, Helen remained at the family home.

The residence was maintained by the Condit family for ninety-eight years, and Helen Condit was the last family member to reside in the home. Helen lived to be eighty-seven years old, passing away on December 10, 1961. Helen is buried with six of her siblings and her parents in the family plot located in section three at Highland Lawn Cemetery. Before her death, Helen made arrangements for Indiana State University to take possession of the home, entrusting the institution with the care and upkeep of the historic home. The university restored and remodeled the residence in 1968, and it was added to the National Register of Historic Places on April 2, 1973. It now stands as the oldest building on the campus of Indiana State University. The Condit House is also recognized as a Historical American Building with the Library of Congress and the Smithsonian Institute.

In the years since Indiana State University received the residence, the Condit House has gained a reputation for the strange activity that occurs within the walls. Many of the stories seem to have occurred during periods when the home was used as offices for the university. I first heard the tales of the Condit House while I attended ISU, when it was being used as office space. With so much sorrow and death in the home, it seems likely that some members of the Condit family may have remained. It is also believed by some that spirits may be more inclined to manifest when restoration or change occurs in their familiar space.

The rumors of ghostly activity at the Condit House include a female spirit that has been seen moving throughout the house. She often moves quickly and is only briefly seen, but some believe that she could be the ghost of Helen. Perhaps she continues to watch over the home she loved so dearly, possibly frowning on the addition of desks and office equipment to the space. It is also possible that the identity of this spirit could be one of the other Condit women who passed in the home, possibly Helen's mother, Sarah, or older sister Emma. Knocking sounds have been heard in the home—almost as if someone is knocking on the door, but when the door is opened, no one is there. Footsteps have also been heard on the stairs inside the home, but much like with the knocking, when someone goes to greet the visitor, they find that no one has entered the home. Other odd noises occur throughout the residence, but they do not seem to have a defined source. It could just be the creaking of an old house, or it could be the spirits of the young Condit children—still playful and somewhat mischievous in the afterlife. The basement door also seems to be a location where ghostly activity occurs. The door has been known to open and close, sometimes even slamming, though it is often locked. While some may question whether the strange activity is paranormal, it is hard to deny that the home has been the location of a great deal of death and despair. That sort of history can leave the home's former inhabitants in a state of limbo. That leads one to wonder: how many long-passed members of the Condit family actually remain at the location?

SAINT MARY-OF-THE-WOODS COLLEGE

3301 SAINT MARY'S ROAD, WEST TERRE HAUTE, INDIANA 47885

Saint Mary-of-the-Woods College, like Indiana State University, began as a college for women. Saint Mary's was originally called the Saint Mary's Female Institute. It is Indiana's oldest Catholic college. In 1840 Saint Mother Theodore Guerin and five other Sisters of Providence traveled from Ruille-sur-Loir, France, to Indiana to establish a college for women. Saint Mother Theodore Guerin was chosen to lead the sisters on the mission to Indiana to assist with the education of Catholic immigrants arriving in the area. Born in the village of Etables-sur-Mer in Brittany, France, on October 2, 1798, as Anne-Therese Guerin, she was forty-two at the time of the trip. She was joined on the voyage by Sister Olympiade Boyer, Sister St. Vincent Ferrer Gagé, Sister Basilide Sénéschal, Sister Mary Xavier Lerée and Sister Mary Liguori Tiercin.

The trip to Indiana took the sisters three months, and despite a stormy ocean voyage and the theft of much of their remaining money, the sisters persevered and finally crossed the Wabash River, arriving in Indiana on October 22, 1840. The area that would become Saint Mary-of-the-Woods was desolate when the sisters arrived, but Saint Mother Theodore was not deterred. She managed to open the school in less than a year—on July 4, 1841. She also helped oversee the construction of the motherhouse for the Sisters of Providence at Saint Mary-of-the-Woods.

Saint Mother Theodore Guerin was an extraordinary woman. After finishing her work at Saint Mary's Female Institute, she continued her mission by opening schools in Indiana and eastern Illinois—some of which still exist today. She also established two free pharmacies in Indiana and two orphanages in Vincennes, Indiana. Saint Mother Theodore had been plagued by health issues for most of her life, and her last bout of illness commenced on March 15, 1856. She passed away nearly two months later on May 14, 1856, at the motherhouse on the grounds of Saint Mary-of-the-Woods. Saint Mother Theodore was originally buried in the Sisters of Providence Cemetery, which was located on a small hill not far from the Saint Anne Shell Chapel on the motherhouse grounds. On December 3, 1907, Saint Mother Theodore's remains were moved from their original resting place to a crypt in the Church of the Immaculate Conception at Saint Mary-of-the-Woods. A Celtic cross now marks the location of her original burial. The cross is inscribed with the words, "I sleep but my heart watches over this house which I have built." Saint Mother Theodore Guerin's story would not end with her passing in 1907.

Saint Mother Theodore Guerin went on to become the United States' eighth saint, following her canonization on October 15, 2006. She was given the official name of Saint Theodora following a ceremony at Saint Peter's Square at the Vatican in Rome, Italy. Mother Theodore was originally declared blessed in 1998 when Pope John Paul II accepted the miraculous healing of one of the Sisters of Providence, Mary Theodosia Mug, in 1908. Sister Mug was a writer and teacher who had written a very well-received book about the life of Saint Mother Theodore Guerin in 1904. Two years later, at the age of forty-six, Sister Mug discovered a lump in her left breast and was diagnosed with malignant cancer. Her physician recommended that she undergo an immediate mastectomy. Seeing no other option, the sister opted to go forward with the procedure. Following the mastectomy, it was discovered that the nerves and muscles on her left side had been damaged during surgery, and her left arm became very stiff. Unfortunately, a lump in her abdomen continued to grow, causing the sister much pain. She was soon unable to kneel, had to eat standing up and would often experience difficulty walking. On the evening of October 30, 1908, Sister Mug was passing by the tomb of Saint Mother Theodore Guerin when she decided to stop and pray for a fellow sister who was very ill. She then returned to her quarters to retire for the evening. Upon waking the following morning, Sister Mug felt better than she had in years. Her left arm was no longer stiff, and the large abdominal tumor had miraculously disappeared. The cancer that once plagued Sister Mug never returned, and she lived to be eighty-two years old, passing away in 1943. This would be the first miracle attributed to Saint Mother Theodore Guerin but not the last.

In 2001 Phillip McCord, a Protestant and the director of facilities management for the Sisters of Providence, found himself dealing with severe vision problems. His doctor at the time recommended that he have surgery performed on both eyes to remove cataracts. The first surgery on the left eye was a success, but the second surgery did not achieve the same result for the right eye. Following that surgery, there were immediate issues with the right eye, including heaviness, drooping eyelid and redness in the face. The discomfort did not heal with further treatment, and another specialist later confirmed that there was swelling in the cornea. Due to the damage in Mr. McCord's eye, the specialist suggested that he undergo cornea transplant surgery on his right eye. Mr. McCord was unsure if he wanted to go forward with such a dangerous procedure, so he decided to pray to Saint Mother Theodore for peace and guidance and for the strength to move forward with the procedure. When he awoke on the morning following his prayer, Mr. McCord realized that the heaviness in his eye had dissipated, and the droopiness seemed to have diminished as well. At this point, he still planned to have the surgery despite the improvements with his eye, but when he met with the specialist, Mr. McCord was shocked to learn that he no longer needed surgery, as his eye was beginning to heal on its own. The only further treatment required was a simple laser procedure to remove some tissue buildup in the eye. Mr. McCord's vision had been restored without any sort of medical intervention. In April 2006, Pope Benedict XVI accepted the healing of Philip McCord as the second miracle required for the canonization of Saint Mother Theodore Guerin, now Saint Theodora.

In the years since Saint Mother Theodore Guerin founded Saint Mary-of-the-Woods, the college has become well-known for its history as well as the beautiful architecture on campus. The college also houses the White Violet Center for eco-justice, which is a rural ministry for the Sisters of Providence. The White Violet Center includes a five-acre certified organic garden, a flock of laying chickens, orchards, a hiking trail, beehives, a farm store and some of the cutest alpacas you've ever seen. Saint Mary-of-the-Woods has also become known as having a reputation as one of the most haunted locations in Terre Haute.

The most famous apparition reported at Saint Mary-of-the-Woods is that of the Faceless Nun. She is believed to be a sister and an artist. The first tales involving the Faceless Nun occurred in Foley Hall, a building that formerly housed the college's art department. Construction began on the building in 1860, with east and west wings added in 1871 and a front section completed in 1897. As the story goes, one of the nuns was a portrait artist and spent many of her days in Foley Hall, perfecting her art. She was meticulous and had a specific order in which she did her portraits, always painting the face last. She was always looking for subjects to paint, but there came a time when she was unable to find a model. Still wanting to pursue her art, the nun decided to paint a self-portrait following the same order as always with the intention of painting the face last. Unfortunately, this was not to be. On the day the nun was to begin work on her own face, she suddenly fell ill. She was immediately taken to the infirmary, where she passed away not long after. As you can imagine, the story of the Faceless Nun does not end there.

Stories have long circulated from students and staff about the strange nun at Saint Mary-of-the-Woods. An early account tells of a sister who heard weeping in Foley Hall. Upon following the sound, she came to the room where the unfinished painting remained. Concerned, the sister entered the room and found another sister mournfully sobbing in front of the painting. She attempted to comfort the distraught sister, but when the sister turned to face her, she was shocked to see that there was nothing but blackness where her face should have been.

The Faceless Nun has also been seen as a shadowy figure floating down the hallways and in the courtyard of Foley Hall. Another early documented account involved an art department employee named Isabel who apparently had several run-ins with the Faceless Nun, even stating on one occasion, "She leaves when I speak to her, and I never see her face." A Mass was eventually held by the sisters to help calm the restless spirit of the Faceless Nun. It is hard to tell if the Mass succeeded, as Foley Hall caught fire and was torn down in 1989.

In the years since the razing of Foley Hall, reports of the Faceless Nun and other strange activity seem to center on the Conservatory of Music, a building that is located right next to where Foley Hall used to be. Construction on the conservatory finished in 1913, and the building is located on the former grounds of the second Saint Mary-of-the-Woods village church and cemetery. The building was dedicated on October 13, 1913, along with another building on campus—Guerin Hall.

The Conservatory of Music at Saint Mary-of-the-Woods College. Strange happenings have occurred in this building. *Courtesy of Elizabeth Christjansen.*

Many people have reported pianos playing in the practice rooms of the conservatory, but when they reach the room, the playing stops. Upon opening the door, they find that no one is inside. Footsteps have also been heard in the hallways, but when one turns to see who is behind them, no one is there. There is also a heavy door in the basement that has shut behind visitors to the conservatory, but upon trying to reenact the event, it seems that the door is not subject to wind and is too heavy to close on its own. One former student I spoke with reported what she believed to be exorcism stickers on some of the door frames throughout the Conservatory of Music. Upon further inspection, I found a strange sticker on a first-floor bathroom during my visit to the conservatory. Though I am not sure of the purpose of the sticker, it is worth noting, considering the history of the former location as a cemetery and the reports that have circulated about the ghostly happenings in the Conservatory of Music.

Anne Therese Guerin Hall was named in honor of Saint Mother Theodore Guerin. The building is not far from the Conservatory of Music. The four-story Renaissance Revival building was originally used as a dormitory with both shared and private rooms but now serves as

The sticker on the bathroom door in the Conservatory of Music at Saint Mary-of-the-Woods College. *Courtesy of Elizabeth Christjansen.*

administrative offices and classrooms for the college. Students and staff have long reported the existence of an entity that behaves much like a poltergeist in the hall. This spirit is often referred to as "three back" or the Dark Angel of Guerin Hall. There is a story of a student who attended the college in the 1930s who would later tell her daughter the tale of a female student who hanged herself in room 334. Oddly, the activity in Guerin Hall seems to center on room 334, which is a corner room on the third floor of the building. Former residents have reported objects moving on their own, strange sounds that can't be explained and even passing shadows when no one else is nearby. The most bizarre report from Guerin Hall is that of a wall-mounted crucifix that was said to have moved from side to side without any outside intervention.

Le Fer Hall is a large French Renaissance Revival–style building that was completed in 1924. It serves as a residence hall and is known for having its share of ghostly activity. One former student I spoke with reported seeing a dark figure in the hallway that followed her for a short distance before disappearing. Other students have reported sightings of a similar shadowy figure in the hallways of Le Fer Hall. Accounts also claim that

Guerin Hall at Saint Mary-of-the-Woods College. Poltergeist-like activity has occurred in this building. *Courtesy of Elizabeth Christjansen.*

Le Fer Hall Saint Mary-of-the-Woods College. A dark figure has been seen roaming the halls of this building. *Courtesy of Elizabeth Christjansen.*

some students have been awoken by the sensation of being touched in their beds only to open their eyes and find that no one is there. This building may also be the home to the Black Bird of Saint Mary-of-the-Woods. The spirit is reported to take a dark form and has been seen on the campus, although once again, not much information is available regarding where the entity has been seen or how it behaves.

FACE IN THE WALL

FORMERLY AT THE INTERSECTION OF FRUITRIDGE AVENUE AND HULMAN STREET, TERRE HAUTE

This is a story that I originally came across during my senior year in high school while doing a yearbook article about Terre Haute's haunted history. Unfortunately, this is one of those stories that may be more myth than truth, but it also serves as a cautionary tale for teens and adults with a need for speed.

Fruitridge Avenue is located in Eastern Vigo County. Though the road is straight, it is very hilly and has seen its share of bad accidents through the years. One such accident involved teenage drag racers out for a good time. I like to envision this event happening in the 1950s, though I'm not really sure when it is reported to have happened.

It is not known who challenged whom, but all accounts claim that the race was going as normal—each car accelerated, racing down Fruitridge Avenue at high speeds until the cars approached a hill just beyond Hulman Street. One of the vehicles blew a tire, and though the driver tried to regain control, he was unable to do so. His vehicle careened from the roadway and crashed. The teen was thrown from the car and landed head first into a rock wall on the east side of the road. As you can imagine, he did not survive the injuries and died as a result.

One might assume that the story ends here, but this story has become a cautionary tale not so much because of the accident itself but because of the story that followed. Not long after the teen's funeral, locals who happened along Fruitridge Avenue at night claimed to see the face of a young man in the wall. Some thought it was the imprint of the boy's face due to the impact of the crash because there would have been a lot of blood, but others believed it could be the spirit of the boy. Local teens soon began to claim that if you approached the wall and put your finger in the center of the face, you would die within twenty-four hours. The claims eventually became too much to ignore and attempts were made to cover the face that haunted the wall, but it always returned. It is believed that someone eventually attempted to scrape the face from the wall, but that did not remedy the issue either. Some people still claim that if you drive on Fruitridge Avenue at night, you might just see the boy's face staring back at you.

Though this story is the most well-known version of the Face in the Wall, other stories have circulated throughout the years in an attempt to explain the anomaly that many folks reported seeing on the wall. One such story tells of a young boy who had lived in the home on the corner of Fruitridge and Hulman. He was playing in the yard with his father when he ran out onto Fruitridge as a concrete truck was passing. The truck struck the boy, killing him instantly. It is said that the driver of the truck was so distraught over the accident that he took some of the concrete and used it to model an image of the dead boy's face on the wall. In this story, it is believed that the face became a stop for local teenagers who had heard the myth and wanted to see the face for themselves.

A similar story states that after the young boy was killed, his parents actually built the wall and created a face out of some of the stones. They placed lights in the eyes as a reminder for the man who had killed the child and to remind others driving down Fruitridge to maintain the proper speed limit and watch for pedestrians.

Still a third version of the story began circulating in the late 1940s. In this version, the story states that the boy was actually hit by a driver that fled following the accident. The driver was never found, so he could not be arrested and tried for his crime. The boy's father, distraught over the loss of his son, painted a face in white paint on the wall. The father hoped that by doing this, the driver who had hit the boy would see the face, causing his conscience to get the best of him and perhaps he would come forward and admit to his crime. In a similar story, the boy was hit by a speeding driver who fled the scene, but instead of the father painting his face on the wall, the story states that the impact of the accident actually launched the child into the wall, leaving the imprint of his face behind.

There is yet another story about a little boy dying, but this is a much darker tale. The boy was reportedly hit by a tractor, and after the incident, the father became so distraught at the loss of his son that he went crazy. He molded an image of son's face out of plaster and placed it on the wall, and he evidently plucked the young boy's eyes from the corpse and placed them in the plaster face. Filled with a need for revenge over the loss of his son, the father then abducted the tractor driver and locked him in a cage within a small shed at the property on Fruitridge Avenue and Hulman Street. The father kept the man there until he died. However, the story does not state what the father did with the man's body or if the father was ever arrested for his crimes.

Still another version of the story that began circulating in the 1960s states that a girl was killed in an accident at the location. Much like the stories of the drag-racing teenagers and the little boy, following the girl's death, a strange face appeared in the wall, prompting local teenagers to visit the site at night, shining their headlights at the wall in an attempt to see the face of the young girl.

There is one final version of the story that includes reports of visitors to the site having encounters with the ghost of a man. As the story goes, this man lost his life as a result of drinking and driving. He had been driving down Fruitridge when he apparently veered off course and hit the wall head-on. The driver was launched through the windshield and slammed his face against the wall. The impact left an imprint of the man's face on the wall that could be seen for several years following his death. Other reports claim that, even today, if you go to the former site of the wall on Fruitridge and Hulman at night, you might just see the ghost of the man looking for his lost face that was long ago washed away from the wall.

HEADLESS TRAINMAN

LOCATION UNKNOWN

G host lights, also known as spook lights, are strange phenomena in which unexplained balls of light, which are visible to the naked eye, are reported. These lights have been witnessed throughout the United States—often associated with ghostly tales of death and loss. The figures at the center of these ghost light stories often experienced a tragic event, and many seem to have lost their heads.

There are many railroad tracks throughout Vigo County, so it makes sense that Terre Haute's spook light is associated with the railroad activity in the area. Though the spook light in neighboring Clay County is well known and frequently visited, such is not the case with Terre Haute's spook light. I attempted to find the exact location, but I could not find any firsthand accounts of the story and I was unable to trace the origins of the tale or even the area involved. Perhaps someone unfamiliar with the legend known as the Headless Trainman will read this chapter and realize that they have seen the reported activity, allowing additional information to be included in the story.

The track in question seems to be located somewhere south of Terre Haute, and the route runs north–south. As the story goes, a freight train was rushing along on its way to Evansville, Indiana. The train was apparently going faster than it should have been for such an old stretch of track. One of the rails holding the track together was quite loose and unable to handle the momentum of the speeding train. When the locomotive entered the area, it hit the loose rail, careened off of the track and crashed. The conductor and brakeman were both killed on impact. When authorities arrived, they found the conductor's lifeless body not far from the wreckage. They were not immediately able to find the body of the brakeman. They scoured the scene, finally finding the man nearby. Rescuers were shocked to discover that the body was missing its head. Over the next few days, police officers and volunteers began clearing the wreckage from the site. They tried their best to find the brakeman's lost head in an attempt to reunite it with the body, but sadly the trainman's head was never found.

Legend states that if you walk near the area of the accident at night or find yourself stopped by a train, you might just see a shadowy figure walking along the south side of the railroad track. Witnesses report, upon closer inspection, seeing a man holding an old lantern. He appears to be swinging the light back and forth as if he is searching for something. Perhaps this is the ghost of that trainman still searching for his lost head.

ROCKY EDGE

ALLENDALE, TERRE HAUTE, INDIANA

ocky Edge was once a beautiful estate. The home was built by Chapman J. Root, the owner of the Root Glass Company. Root was born in Pennsylvania on November 22, 1864, and he traveled to Terre Haute in 1899 with his wife, Agnes, and established the glass company. Within a year of the couple's arrival, Agnes gave birth to a son, William Ruffle Root, born on September 17, 1900. This must have been quite a happy time for the family and they could only look forward to more success in Terre Haute. Root was a member of the Terre Haute Masonic Lodge, Number Nineteen, as well as a member of the Knights Templar and Scottish Rite Masonic Consistory of Indianapolis. He also served as a Trustee for the Zorah Shrine Temple of Terre Haute. Chapman Root gained fame for inventing the green glass Coca-Cola bottle, which is an iconic design still in use today. As one can imagine, this innovative bottle also earned Root quite a bit of wealth.

In 1925 Chapman Root purchased the eighty-eight-acre Rocky Edge as a weekend retreat. Other articles state that he bought the property in 1920 and waited some years before constructing the home at the site. The residence and surrounding grounds are hidden away from the hustle and bustle of Highway 41 in an area of Terre Haute known as Allendale. This community is known for its beauty, as it sits on a bluff overlooking Honey Creek. Many of the homes were built between the 1920s and 1960s, and Allendale was favored by many members of Terre Haute's early upper class. The area provided scenic views with curvy roads, densely wooded acreage and deep ravines. Local distiller Fred B. Smith once lived in Allendale, later selling his home to the Knights of Columbus. The organization would later found the Gibault School, a home for wayward boys, on the property.

Chapman J. Root's weekend villa is an example of Spanish Revival architecture. The home would have been quite grand in its day with its landscaping of rock gardens and fountains. Rocky Edge served as a location for Root to host guests, so it was outfitted with the finest features. The pool area was surrounded by glass and included painted murals and a fireplace. Visitors could also enjoy the ornate greenhouse or take a stroll through the small zoo located on the property. The interior of the home was a maze of small rooms and hallways with multiple stairways leading to other locations within the residence. There was even a special staircase reserved for the guests of Rocky Edge, allowing them to access the festivities in the pool area. The home also included several bedrooms, a gatehouse, an outdoor sauna, a ballroom and even a bar area. Prohibition-era debauchery is also thought to have occurred at the Root villa, and one former partygoer reportedly stated, "The only thing that went on at Rocky Edge was sex and spirits." Some have even reported strange underground tunnels at Rocky Edge, leading many to wonder if the estate was also used to move bootleg liquor during Prohibition. Though the Root family experienced many happy times when they owned the villa, they were not immune to tragedy. William died on June 23, 1932, when the airplane that he was flying crashed in a field near Farmersburg. Paul S. Cox, a Terre Haute pilot, was also killed in the accident. William Root was only thirty-one. His body was interred in the Root mausoleum in section one at Highland Lawn Cemetery.

Agnes Root died on December 8, 1943. Chapman Root lived another two years following his wife's death, succumbing to complications from diabetes on November 20, 1945. They were both interred in the family mausoleum along with William. The Root family maintained ownership of the home until the 1960s, but it never regained its Prohibition-era glory. In the years since, the once magnificent villa has fallen into utter disrepair, leading it to be known as a location where visitors can experience spirits of another kind. The home has become a favorite spot for both local teenagers looking for a ghostly scare and vandals intent on doing more damage to the estate. The pool area and greenhouse have been reclaimed by Mother Nature with vines dangling from the framework of each building. Much of the glass and tile that once adorned the pool has been lost to time or destruction by vandals. However, much of the structure of the home remains intact.

There is no doubt that the current state of Rocky Edge has contributed to the tales that circulate among local teenagers. The home has taken on the look of a location that might be featured in a horror film, oddly enough probably with teenagers venturing out to an old abandoned house in an attempt to look for ghosts. I must also add that the home is still private property and trespassing of any kind is not allowed. Also, with the current state of the villa, some areas may be unsafe and ghost hunting at the site should be avoided. Despite the decaying condition of the retreat, rumors have started to circulate about shadows moving in the tunnels beneath the home. If the stories about liquor being moved through the tunnels are true, perhaps these are the spirits of former bootleggers who spent their time in the subterranean section of the estate. The sound of movement has also been reported in the tunnels, but in some cases, this is likely the result of small animals that may have found their way into the area. Shadows and ectoplasmic mists have also been spotted near the pool and in locations inside the home, sometimes scaring teenagers and making them flee the property. Strange noises have been reported by people who visit Rocky Edge at night. Footsteps have been heard in the pool area and on the spiral staircase nearby. This would have been a high-traffic location during the parties at the Root villa. It is possible that what people are hearing and seeing in this former gathering place is actually a residual haunting—the energy of so many spirited and gleeful parties having left its mark on Rocky Edge.

The former weekend retreat of Chapman J. Root is currently on the market. It has also been added to the Indiana Landmarks' Top Ten List of Endangered Locations. The villa is just waiting for the right owner to restore the retreat to its original state of grandeur. It would make a wonderful private residence or a lovely bed-and-breakfast. If the stories are true, perhaps the renovations to the estate would fully awaken the ghosts of Rocky Edge, allowing them to welcome the first new guests to the home in decades.

BLUE HOLE

PRAIRIETON, INDIANA, VIGO COUNTY

I discovered this story many moons ago while doing research at the Vigo County Historical Society. It was tucked away in a manila folder of articles that the staff had been kind enough to let me browse through. This long-circulated legend is about a body of water called the Blue Hole near Prairieton, Indiana. For some, the name Blue Hole conjures up images of cheesy monster movies or dangerous bottomless bodies of water. In the case of Vigo County's Blue Hole, tales show that both could be true. Though there is no history to support any of the legends associated with the Blue Hole, the stories are still quite interesting and worth mentioning when discussing the dark and haunted history of Terre Haute.

Blue Holes are typically considered a karst feature. They are created when exposed soluble rock, such as limestone, becomes exposed—usually due to a drop in water level. The exposed material is then eroded by acidic groundwater and rain, which enters through open faults. This can result in cavities, caverns and underground tunnels that eventually weaken the structure of the stone until it collapses in on itself and forms a sinkhole. These sinkholes, also called cenotes, can also occur in areas where coal has been mined.

In the area of Prairieton, Indiana, not far from Terre Haute, there is a three-acre lake with many myths and legends attached to it. Those stories have earned it the reputation of being a Blue Hole. One of the earliest legends tells of pirates who hid their treasure in and around the Blue Hole. In an attempt to protect the treasure, the pirates secured a series of traps around the perimeter of the site, killing anyone who dared to steal their hidden prize.

Other myths about the Blue Hole claim that it is a bottomless body of water and that anything that goes in will never be found again. Such is the case with the story of a lost busload of children. No one knows if they were heading to or from school, but all of the stories agree that when the bus driver crossed the bridge above the Blue Hole, something went terribly wrong and the bus careened from the bridge into the water below. It is claimed that the lake was searched, but no bodies or a bus were ever found. The mother of one of the children visited the site every day following the accident, hoping that the bus would resurface so she could bury her lost daughter. After several months, the mother passed away as a result of her sorrow. The ghost of the grief-stricken mother is reported to manifest as a strange light that moves around within the Blue Hole. Some believe that she still searches for her missing daughter in the afterlife. Another story replaces the busload of children with a train engine. In this case, the engine was believed to have jumped the tracks, sending the train along with the engineer and several workers into the bottomless Blue Hole—never to be seen again.

The Blue Hole is also reportedly haunted by the spirits of a group of boys who drowned at the site. Legend states that the boys had heard the stories of things disappearing into the Blue Hole. In an attempt to disprove the myths, they decided to go for a swim. When the boys did not arrive home as expected, their parents went to the Blue Hole to find their sons—likely to read them the riot act for their tardiness. Instead, all they found were the items of clothing the boys had shed before diving into the Blue Hole. In the years since, stories have circulated about ghostly boys chasing visitors from the site in an attempt to save them from the same fate experienced by the young men so many years before.

The Blue Hole has also been linked to Terre Haute's days as Sin City. It is rumored that gangsters from Chicago would travel to Terre Haute, sometimes opting to use the Blue Hole to make those who had defied them or posed a threat disappear. Considering the rumors regarding Al Capone's visits to the Terre Haute House, this actually seems like one of the more plausible tales of the Blue Hole. However, no deceased mobsters have been pulled from the Blue Hole. Another such story tells of a bootlegger who fell out of favor with his associates. As a result of the disagreement, they shot him to death, later dropping his body in the Blue Hole to conceal their crime.

The final legend regarding the Blue Hole is that of a lake monster. Fishermen and residents in the area have long claimed to see either a Nessie-like creature or a catfish the size of a bus. While it is possible that a monster of that magnitude could survive in the Blue Hole, it would likely require a steady diet of schoolchildren and mob informants. It is doubtful that the Blue Hole is the home of an undocumented Hoosier Hattie, as the creature has never been photographed, and no proof of her existence has ever been found. As for the people and vehicles that have gone missing, if the stories have a grain of truth, it is likely that an underground stream flows beneath the Blue Hole, which could account for anything that might go missing.

SERENDIPITY SALON

823 OHIO STREET,
TERRE HAUTE, INDIANA 47807

When driving down Ohio Street in Terre Haute, one might miss the unassuming brick home near the corner of Ninth Street and Ohio. The house stands two stories tall and includes both Italianate and Queen Anne architectural elements. It was built in 1880 by Gottlieb Reiss. He and his wife, Anna, arrived in Terre Haute by canalboat in 1848. Gottlieb first worked at a hotel on North Third Street before acquiring a position at a local grocery store. He and Anna lived above the grocery store with their burgeoning family before moving to the property at 823 Ohio Street.

In all, Gottlieb and Anna had six children: oldest son John, daughters Caroline, Mary and Rosa and twins George and Emma. Sadly, Emma never had the opportunity to live in the family home, as she passed away on October 4, 1862, at two years and nine months old. It is unclear what caused Emma's passing, but it is possible that she passed in a similar manner to the young Condit children, likely a victim of one of the many infectious diseases that were common at the time. Emma would not be the only Reiss child to pass at an early age.

The Reisses' youngest child, Rosa, passed away on November 19, 1901. Though she was only thirty-three, Rosa, or Rose as she was called, contracted typhoid fever and died as a result of the disease, leaving behind two young sons—one three years old and the other just fifteen months old. Though their father was still alive, the children were left in the care of Rose's older sister, Carrie, also known as Caroline. Carrie remained at the home at 823 Ohio Street her entire life, raising the boys there. She never married, and she treated the boys as if they were her own. George, Emma's twin, who at the time was known as the "oldest acting druggist in the state," moved into the home with Carrie when they reached their golden years. They would be the last members of the Reiss family to reside in the home, with George passing away on December 20, 1941. After George died, Carrie was no longer able to live alone in the home. She split her time between two of her nieces—six months each. Carrie outlived George by seven years, passing away on October 19, 1948, at ninety-one.

Gottlieb and Anna's other daughter, Mary, was born in 1862 and was the fourth child in the family. She passed away at the age of seventy-four following a bout with breast cancer. John Reiss, born in 1855, became a well-known businessman. He was also known for dabbling in politics. He was stricken with sudden blindness in 1930. Eight years later, John underwent eye surgery to correct his blindness, but the surgery was not successful. John passed away on October 25, 1838. It is thought that his death was a result of complications from the eye surgery. All of the members of the Reiss family are buried at Woodlawn Cemetery with the exception of John and Mary, who are both buried with their spouses at Highland Lawn Cemetery.

After the passing of George and Carrie Reiss, the home was purchased by William Van Horn, a local dentist. He served in World War II, and upon returning to Terre Haute after the war, he converted the home into a private dental practice. The property would function as the Van Horn Dental Office for decades, with Van Horn's son, Peter, joining the practice in 1973. William practiced at the location until his retirement in 1983. It was in that same year, on June 30, 1983, that the home was added to the National Register of Historic Places. The dental practice served the city of Terre Haute for many years following William's retirement before the home was sold once again in 2015.

The former home is currently the location of Serendipity Salon. The salon offers upscale beauty services in a historic and beautiful setting. Serendipity Salon differs from most salons in that beyond the services that it offers, clients may also experience an encounter with a ghost. Since moving into the building in 2015, many of the stylists, including Serendipity Salon owner Cheryl Salyers, have reported interacting with a ghost girl they fondly refer to as Annie. Cheryl was kind enough to allow one of my haunted history tour groups access to the salon. The house is typical of a home built in the 1880s with beautiful woodwork and a twisting staircase leading to the second floor. The home has been kept in pristine condition—some areas give visitors the feeling that they have stepped back in time. Cheryl shared a bit of the history and haunts of the home with the tour group and reported that there is a door leading to what appears to be a tunnel beneath the home. Cheryl has not ventured into the mysterious tunnel, but I sincerely hope that curiosity gets the best of her soon. It would be interesting to know what is located beneath the former Reiss residence.

Cheryl believes that Annie is a young girl, perhaps in her twenties or early thirties, and that she died tragically. One former tenant of the building's second floor reported hearing light footfalls as if a child were walking around the building. Items in her office were also reportedly manipulated and moved, though not far from where she left the items. She further reported feeling that the ghost was that of a playful young girl. Annie has been known to move small things and make knocking sounds. Employees in the building have also experienced strange cold spots. Though she likes to make herself known, the spirit of Annie seems to be very playful, and she doesn't cause any trouble.

Rose Reiss seems to be a likely suspect for the spirit that makes her home at Serendipity Salon. Rose died quite young, and with her boys left in the care of Carrie, it is likely that the children spent a great deal of time at 823 Ohio Street. It is also likely that Rose was still living with her family when

The former Reiss residence and present-day location of Serendipity Salon. The spirit of a girl is drawn to this home. *Courtesy of Elizabeth Christjansen.*

they moved to the home, so she probably would have lived in the residence as a teenager. Since Rose died when her boys were merely toddlers, Rose's spirit could have been drawn to her young children and the familiarity of the home. Some of the activity experienced could certainly be attributed to that of a young lady. The knocking and the cold spots seem to indicate that the spirit is trying to make itself known.

But what if the ghost is that of a young child? Emma Reiss seems to be the only young child associated with the home to have passed away. Though she did not die on the grounds, she was George's twin sister. The bond between twins is thought to be quite strong, so perhaps Emma Reiss maintained that bond with George in the afterlife. Though George did not spend his entire life in the home, he did live there for several years until his death in 1941. Similar to Rosa's potential reasons for remaining on the grounds, it was the family home, and young Emma may have chosen to follow her family and twin brother into their new residence. The movement of small items and the playful behavior of the spirit does lend to that of a child. With the varying activity, perhaps it is possible that both Emma and Rose remain at the home, both having died well before their time and both sharing strong bonds with those they left behind. One thing is for certain: the ghost referred to as Annie is most likely a long-passed member of the Reiss family still connected with the property that her family called home for sixty-eight years.

MARKLE MILL SITE
OR "OLD MILL DAM"

4945–5099 MILL DAM ROAD,
NORTH TERRE HAUTE, INDIANA 47805

This is the place where my mother preferred that I not "look" for ghosts when I was a teenager. She held the belief that not only was Mill Dam haunted but that it was also a location where bad things tended to happen. This was mostly due to the rapidly flowing water at the site. The wide, deep pool of water below the dam is also known as a good fishing site, but it is dangerous and swimming is forbidden. In the years since my mother warned me about Mill Dam, I have come to appreciate the site not only for its ghost tales but also for the history and beauty of the location.

Major Abraham Markle came to Terre Haute in 1816, the year Indiana became a state. Markle was a gentleman with quite a storied past. He had been a member of the Canadian Parliament when Canada was a British province. When the War of 1812 broke out, Markle sided with the United States, opting to lead a group of his fellow dissenters across Canada, setting fire to the towns and villages they passed through. Markle went on to serve in the United States Army, earning the rank of major. Markle was deemed a traitor in his home country of Canada and was tried for his crimes but was not even present for the proceedings. Markle was convicted and sentenced to death by hanging, with the added stipulation that he would be "hanged by the neck but not until you are dead, for you must be cut down while alive and your entrails taken out and burned before your face." Clearly, the time had come for Markle to flee Canada.

By leaving his home behind, Markle was forced to abandon roughly 1,500 acres of land. Considering he had supported the United States during the war, Markle decided to petition Congress for land grants in the Harrison Purchase on the Wabash River for Canadian volunteers. Markle was given permission to take possession of 4,200 acres of land on what is now called Otter Creek on March 5, 1816. By July of that year, Markle and two associates, Joseph Richardson and Daniel Stringham, had traveled from Olean, New York, to the site in present-day North Terre Haute. He helped form the Terre Haute Land Company, a group that was instrumental in the platting of the village of Terre Haute in 1816. Markle also had experience building mills in Canada, so he immediately got to work constructing a combination saw/grist mill and corn whiskey distillery. Markle enlisted the help of a local mechanic and wheelwright, Ezra Jones, for his skills on the mill, and the project was completed in 1817. When finished, the mill was quite a sight. The foundation and accompanying dam included three limestone archways, allowing the waters of the creek to turn the mill's wooden water wheel. The structure above was constructed from wood cut from trees near the creek and was three stories high.

The mill was the center of activity for local farmers who needed their wares ground into grain. Markle gained a license to sell merchandise and added a general store to the site, allowing him to further furnish supplies for his customers. The general store sold items including eggs, whiskey, sugar and tea. However, customers could also purchase boards and nails for coffins. Markle was known to be a quite a colorful man, involving himself with politics but also finding himself in a few scuffles with other local men. He was even known to be the defendant in several assault and battery cases. Markle ran his mill and general store without fail until his sudden passing on March 26, 1826, ten short years after constructing the mill on Otter Creek. Markle is buried in the Markle family cemetery located on Fruitridge Avenue, roughly one-fourth mile south of the intersection of Fruitridge and Park Avenue. Markle failed to create a will prior to his death, causing much chaos for the heirs to his estate. His heirs eventually lost some of Markle's property due to a foreclosure on 320 acres near present-day downtown Terre Haute. The mill was awarded to the family, and Markle's son Fredrick took over control of the mill.

A series of upgrades was made to the mill under Fred Markle. The wooden dam was lengthened to span the entire creek, allowing the full flow of the creek to power the mill. The dam also included a tunnel for workers to crawl through so they could inspect the dam when necessary. Fred used land across the street from the mill to build a home for his family in 1848. The home, now known as the Markle House, was constructed in Greek Revival style with four fireplaces throughout the three-story home. The Markle home still stands today and is reported to have its fair share of strange and ghostly activity. The home has a stone foundation with a brick exterior and still contains the original woodwork, interior doors and a period staircase. Fred kept an office in the Markle House and ran mill operations from there.

The Civil War broke out in 1861, and Markle's Mill is thought to have played a key role in Underground Railroad activity in Terre Haute. The mill housed ammunition during the war and was also the headquarters of the home guard, of which Fredrick Markle was the commanding officer. Slaves fleeing Virginia, North Carolina and South Carolina traveled to Vigo County, where there was a small settlement of freed slaves, Native Americans and Quakers living together peacefully in Lost Creek Township. The escaping slaves were given shelter throughout the county. Runaway slaves were rumored to be hidden in the Markle House, the inspection tunnel of the dam and in tunnels beneath the mill. It is also likely that slaves were hidden in a small cave system in the woods behind the mill. Visitors to the caves in the woods have found pieces of clothing and cooking utensils in the caves, further supporting the belief that the site could have been a stop on the Underground Railroad. The escaping slaves would remain hidden in Vigo County until they could be guided to Cass County, Michigan, and from there safely into Canada. Despite the conflict of the Civil War, a lack of manpower and the possibility that the mill was harboring escaping slaves, the Markle Mill continued with business as usual, never missing a day of production from 1861 to 1865.

Fred maintained ownership of the mill until his death on October 12, 1866, leaving the mill to his sons, William and Frederick. The Markle sons only ran the mill for twenty-two years before selling the business in 1888 to John Creal, who after a time sold the mill to T.J. Welch. The final owner, C.D. Hansel, purchased the mill in 1910. Hansel collected artifacts and history of the mill, keeping his collection in his office at the mill. Hansel made further upgrades to the site beyond those that had been done by Fred Markle years earlier. The dam was upgraded to concrete, and the wooden water wheel was replaced with a metal turbine. In 1935 Hansel installed a steam engine to power the roller mill, while still using the power of Otter Creek to fuel his corn mill.

The remains of the former Markle Mill. Many paranormal occurrences have been reported here over the years. *Courtesy of Elizabeth Christjansen.*

By 1938 the mill had been running consistently for 121 years and had earned the reputation of being both the "Oldest Mill West of the Alleghenies" and the "Longest-Operating Grist Mill East of the Mississippi River." Hansel's upgrades allowed the mill to run twenty-four hours a day, but tragedy was on the horizon. On September 20, 1938, two millworkers smelled the obvious aroma of smoke. Upon further investigation, they found the upper floor of the mill engulfed in flames. The fire department rushed to the scene, but the old timber provided ample feed for the fire and the mill burned rapidly. Large sections of the mill broke loose and fell into Otter Creek. When the smoke cleared, the wooden portion of the mill had been completely destroyed along with Hansel's collection of historical items related to the mill. All that remained to serve as a reminder of Markle's Mill was the concrete arches of the foundation and the dam itself. After the fire Anton Hulman Jr. purchased the site, and in 1967 the property, including the foundation and dam, was made into a public park. Visitors can now enjoy the beauty of the site. The former mill site and Fred Markle's home were added to the National Register of Historic Places on September 10, 1979.

In the years since, Old Mill Dam—as it is often called by locals—has become a place of interest for ghost hunters due to the reports of strange nighttime activity at the site. The dam has been the site of many drownings in the past. One of the earliest reported deaths at the site occurred in July 1933, when seven-year-old John Dean of Brazil, Indiana, drowned in Otter Creek, just above the dam. It is also possible that slaves may have perished on the site as they awaited the next leg of their journey to freedom. That seems to be the origin story of the most commonly reported ghostly presence at the site.

Legend says that in the days of the Underground Railroad, a group of slaves was being hidden in the tunnels on the site. There was a small girl with the group, and being curious as children often are, she wandered out of the tunnels to get a closer look at the fast-moving water. Unfortunately, she got too close to the edge of Otter Creek and fell in. Her small body was quickly swept over the dam into the pool below where she drowned. The story does not state whether the child's body was ever recovered. The spirit of this little girl is frequently seen by visitors to Old Mill Dam. She is often seen standing near the edge of Otter Creek, likely the last place she stood before falling into the raging torrent of water. It has been reported that when walking along the edge of the bank, visitors have witnessed wet footprints appear, as if a small child is walking along beside them. The little ghost girl is thought to be very particular regarding who can visit the park. She has been said to appear to visitors that she does not like and firmly tells them to "go away." I have also heard reports of electronic voice phenomena (EVP) being captured at the site, but I have not had an opportunity to listen to any of the audio that has supposedly been collected at the site. Though the spirit of the little girl seems to be the most encountered ghost at Old Mill Dam, she certainly isn't alone.

Full-body apparitions have been seen on the grounds of the former mill, as well as near the creek. Visitors often believe they see a person moving in the dark, but upon closer examination, they find that no one is there. Strange swirling mists known as ectoplasm have been witnessed lingering over and near the creek, and one spirit is said to take the form of a woman hovering over the creek. Visitors have witnessed strange lights bouncing around in the woods near the dam. With a busy road, a railroad crossing and a railroad bridge nearby, many are inclined to attribute the strange lights to vehicles and trains. However, orbs have also been spotted with the naked eye and photographed at the site, with many claiming that Old Mill Dam is a hotspot for paranormal encounters. Regardless of what people are seeing at the site, with so much activity reported over the years, it is hard to deny the existence of something strange at the Old Mill Dam.

PRESTON HOUSE

FORMERLY 1339 POPLAR STREET, TERRE HAUTE, INDIANA

On a busy section of Poplar Street, just east of where the road intersects with Thirteenth Street and turns from mostly businesses to residential homes, one might be surprised to see an empty lot surrounded by a tall chainlink fence. This was once the location of one of Terre Haute's oldest and finest homes, the Preston House, which is thought to hold many secrets. Construction on the Preston House began on September 22, 1823, though it would not be finished until 1826. The home was built by Major George Dewees for $20,000, which was quite a sum at the time. Dewees had moved with his wife, Matilda, and young son to Terre Haute from New Orleans in 1822. It was reported that he had made a fortune as a slave trader while living in the South.

Major Dewees modeled his new home in Terre Haute on the Southern Plantation style that would have been common in New Orleans at that time. The first floor of the home was half above and half below the ground level and contained living spaces for the family. The second floor was built six feet above ground level with three large rooms and a central hallway. The outside of the house was adorned with a long staircase and beautiful veranda, a common design decision for homes built in the Southern Plantation style. Dewees's design choice may have seemed like an odd architectural decision for a home in Terre Haute, but many agree that the home was quite stunning. It was situated on 160 acres far from the center of town with two large dogs that regularly kept watch, ensuring that Dewees and his family could live a life of solitude, rarely troubled by visitors.

Vintage image of the Preston House. Sadly, the home no longer stands. *Courtesy of the Vigo County Historical Society.*

Many reports claim that Dewees was an ill-tempered and angry man given to fits of rage. However, it seems he was respected enough to operate a general store on South Second Street and to later become president of the public library. He also held stock in the Terre Haute branch of the Second State Bank of Indiana. Unfortunately, the happiness the Dewees family experienced in their new hometown would be short-lived, eventually leading to the first dark tale to circulate about the Preston House. Sometime between 1827 and 1832, the family would be dealt their first tragedy. Reportedly, George and Matilda's young son was taken by a group of Native Americans and was later found scalped. Surely the death of their young son had to take a toll on George and Matilda's marriage, and it was soon reported that the couple began to argue frequently and were seen less and less about town. In 1932 Matilda decided that she had enough of her marriage to George and filed for divorce, which was not common for women to do at the time. On March 15, 1932, Matilda and George signed a decree stating that they would live apart. George later claimed that following the signing of the decree, Matilda had left Terre Haute to visit family.

That would be the last time anyone saw Matilda Dewees. Rumors began to circulate that perhaps George, in a fit of rage over the divorce, had killed Matilda, but if so, what had become of her body? It is said that in the upstairs area of the house, there were two rooms with identical fireplaces. On each side of the fireplace in the west room were matching cupboards, but in the east room, there was only one cupboard and the opposite side of the fireplace had been covered in bricks from floor to ceiling. Many came to believe that this location next to the fireplace was the final resting place of Matilda Dewees. On April 14, 1832, barely a month after Matilda's disappearance, George put the property up for sale. The months came and went, but there was still no sign of Matilda. George remained on the property—his anger still very much evident.

On election day, November 7, 1832, George was arrested, not for Matilda's murder, but for the attempted murder of Captain James Wasson. The two men had gotten in an argument over politics, and Dewees shot Wasson in the back. Wasson recovered from his injuries, prompting a Parke County jury to find Dewees guilty of only assault and battery. He was sentenced to pay a mere $50 fine and $61.91 in court fees, but Dewees's penchant for violence was now more obvious than ever. Some say karma caught up with the ill-tempered major when he fell ill in the winter of 1832, prompting his niece Elizabeth Patterson to travel from Philadelphia to Terre Haute to care for him. George Dewees would linger for another two years, finally passing away on November 29, 1834. George made no mention of Matilda in his will, instead he left half of the home and grounds to his niece Elizabeth and the other half to his sister, Ann Potts, who lived in Philadelphia. Before Elizabeth and Ann could lay claim to the property, the authorities had to ensure that Matilda had no interest in her former home. A suit was brought forth on Matilda's behalf by William Early, an executor of the will, but Matilda did not appear as requested. Many wondered what had happened to her. On October 29, 1835, William Early received a letter, supposedly from Matilda, releasing her claim to the home. Many found this strange, considering no one had seen or heard from Matilda in almost four years. A later story also circulated that Matilda had been seen in France, but no evidence was ever brought forth to prove that claim. Further evidence suggests that Matilda had actually gone back to New Orleans, where in 1836 her name was signed to a bill of sale for two slaves, and the document was formally recorded in 1837. Matilda would never be seen in Terre Haute again, leaving many to speculate as to what had actually become of her.

The story of the Preston House does not end with the tale of the Dewees family. Though George's sister and niece retained ownership of the home until 1843, it is unclear as to who, if anyone, was actually living in the home during that time. Legend states that George outfitted his home with one additional architectural oddity: tunnels beneath the foundation. It is uncertain what purpose the tunnels might have originally served, but following George's death, the tunnels found new use as a stop on the Underground Railroad. Many fleeing slaves reportedly passed safely through the tunnels of the Preston House until one fateful day when things did not go as planned. The tunnels were full of people awaiting the chance to move on to their next stop. As the story goes, the tunnel collapsed that day, trapping several people beneath the entrance to the home. No attempt was made to save the victims of the collapse for fear that doing so would alert neighbors to the home's use on the Underground Railroad. As a result, everyone in the tunnel died. In the years following the tunnel collapse, particularly in the home's later years, rumors began to circulate regarding strange activity in the home and on the grounds. Visitors have reported hearing the ghostly sound of singing, describing it as the spirituals that were often sung by slaves as an expression of their desire to escape bondage.

The Preston House was purchased by its namesake, Nathaniel Preston, for $6,000 in March 1843. Preston worked as a cashier at the Terre Haute branch of the Second State Bank of Indiana. He raised four children in the home, seemingly unphased by the dark tales that haunted the home. The family maintained the residence for 130 years. Nathaniel Preston's granddaughter, Natalie Preston-Smith, was the final resident of the Preston House. Natalie lived in the home for many years, but as she aged, she was unable to tend to such a large home. She moved to the Terre Haute House in her later years but took a taxi to the Preston House every day so she could feed and care for her cats. Natalie passed away on May 31, 1973, at the age of ninety-four.

In her will she left her personal belongings and all items within the home to the Daughters of the American Revolution, and the home itself was given to Richard Van Allen, the manager of the Terre Haute House. Many hoped that the Daughters of the American Revolution would purchase the home, thereby maintaining the original furnishings and the history of the home. However, the Preston House remained under the ownership of Van Allen and his wife. The couple made minor repairs to the home, but it remained vacant for six years, likely contributing to the home's decline. In November 1979, a rash of fires occurred in vacant homes in the area of Thirteenth and Poplar. It is believed that these fires were started under suspicious circumstances. On November 14, 1979, the Preston House became the next home to fall victim to arson. Though the fire did not destroy the home, vandals and several other fires took their toll. The Preston House remained standing until 1987 when it finally collapsed,

161 years after its construction. It is said that the portion that collapsed was the room where Matilda's body was located. Despite the dark tales surrounding the Preston House, workers clearing the site reported finding no evidence of bones or tunnels. But after years of fires and a collapse, would there be any evidence left to find?

GLENN HOME

7140 WABASH AVENUE,
TERRE HAUTE, INDIANA 47803

T ake a short drive to the outskirts of Terre Haute, and you will find the former location of the Vigo County Home for Dependent Children, or Glenn Home, as it would become known. The home sits on a hill overlooking Highway 40. The location is accessible by a road on the north side of the highway that was an original section of the National Road. The site is only visible in the winter months when the trees surrounding it have lost their leaves. I drove by the property for several years without ever knowing what it was or the history and haunts that it holds.

The origins of the Glenn Home date back to 1901 when Vigo County purchased the sixty-acre Klatte Farm east of Terre Haute. The city was already home to the Rose Orphan Home, which opened its doors to the orphaned youth of Terre Haute in 1884. The Glenn Home would be different. It was created to be a home for Vigo County's abused, neglected and unwanted children. The home would be built according to the "Cottage Plan," which was a common style of asylum-planning used in the early 1900s. This style was known for its use of multiple buildings with individual buildings separating children by age group or gender. The buildings were often no more than two stories tall and made with fireproof materials. The former dorm for African American children, however, burned in the years since the home closed. It was located down a dirt path on the west side of the grounds, and the shell of the building has been overtaken by trees and moss but is still accessible by a small concrete staircase.

The Glenn Home was touted to be one of the best homes for children in the state. When it opened its doors in the summer of 1903, the home included Georgian Revival architecture with an administration building, three dormitories and a boiler house that supplied heat for the entire complex. Children who stayed at the Glenn Home would attend school for half a day and then spend their time learning a useful skill. Boys worked on the grounds of the home's self-sustaining farm, tending to the animals and growing vegetables. Girls would learn skills such as sewing and baking. The employees of the Glenn Home tried to make life as stable as possible for the children. They were well fed and given clean linens and regular healthcare. Students were granted access to a lovely swimming pool and could engage in activities such as horseback riding and tennis.

The home continued to grow, and there was soon a need for the construction of additional buildings. A gymnasium was added in 1926 and still stands to this day. It was often used for sporting activities and for Christmas celebrations, including visits from Santa. The three original dormitories would be razed and replaced with three new dormitories in 1949, all identical in their layout. The dormitory immediately to the east of the administration building was called Leach, and the dormitory to the northeast of Leach was called Alden. The final dormitory sat to the west of the administration building and was referred to as Owen. These buildings should have been a welcome addition to the Glenn Home, but in the years following their construction, other sections of the campus began to fall into disrepair and a source of good water became a constant challenge. By the 1960s, the number of residents at the Glenn Home had dropped significantly. The decline was partly due to the number of licensed foster homes available for misplaced youth, and time had not been kind to the Glenn Home. The once-new dormitories were in need of updated toilet and shower facilities, as well as new floor tile, and many rooms needed to be repainted. These issues would signal the beginning of the end for the Glenn Home.

Reports vary regarding the treatment of the youth housed at the Glenn Home during its last twenty years of operation. Many former residents maintain that they were treated well during their time at the Glenn Home, but other accounts offer a much darker story, detailing instances of mental, physical and sexual abuse. Some stories even claim that children were locked in isolation when they misbehaved or were difficult to deal with. In 1973 it was discovered that the Glenn Home had not renewed its license since 1964 due to what were deemed as

The interior of the Glenn Home gymnasium. *Courtesy of Elizabeth Christjansen.*

"substandard living conditions." The children were found to be living in crowded dormitories with insufficient bathroom facilities. It was also noted in a report by the Terre Haute League of Women Voters that the dormitories were in need of additional fire prevention equipment, along with additional required safety measures. At that time, the League attempted to step in to improve the conditions at the Glenn Home. It requested additional funds from the City Council that would be used to correct some of the issues plaguing the Glenn Home, but a local judge would order the closure of the Glenn Home that same year, stating that renovation of the campus "was impractical." The Glenn Home continued to operate for an additional six years, even receiving some federal funds in 1978. In 1979 the City of Terre Haute purchased three group homes, and the last residents had been moved from the Glenn Home by Christmas 1979.

That would not be the end of the story for the property that once housed so many of Terre Haute's youth. The land was sold in an auction in 1980, and the buildings were used as apartments for a brief time before most of the property was once again abandoned. It would remain that way until the Iota Delta Chapter of Pi Kappa Alpha at

Rose-Hulman Institute of Technology stepped in to breathe new life into the former Glenn Home. The fraternity initially rented only the front section of the administration building, and the first brothers moved to the property in 1987. At that time, the owner of the property also rented the back portion of the house to the state penal system, allowing a group of "work release inmates" to reside there. The inmates would be gone by 1989, allowing the fraternity to lease, and finally purchase, twenty-three acres of the former Glenn Home property in 1993. In the years since purchasing the property, fraternity brothers have become very familiar with the history of the Glenn Home and possibly even some of its ghostly former residents. It is important to note that the former Glenn Home site is on private property, so please respect the wishes of Pi Kappa Alpha and do not trespass on the property.

The only original buildings from 1903 that remain on the site are the administration building and the remains of the former boiler house. Both buildings are on the National Register of Historic Places. The boiler house caught fire a few years ago, but the smokestack remains intact, as does the outer structure of the building. The three cottage-style dormitories and

The burned-out remains of the Glenn Home boiler house. *Courtesy of Elizabeth Christjansen.*

the building for African American youth also remain, but the condition of each building varies—the latter remains a burned-out shell. The fraternity has renovated the former gymnasium and uses the venue for basketball and dodgeball.

The administration building would have originally served as the staff residences and administrative offices. It is a two-and-a-half-story brick building with space in the attic that may have been used to house children. The stairways are quite low when ascending to the upper floor. The exterior of the building is quite stunning, with four white columns supporting a semicircular portico. Due to the building's status on the National Register of Historic Places, the brick is to remain unaltered. A hospital was added to the rear of the administration building, and sick children would have been tended to in that location. There is a cemetery located deep in the woods where children who passed away at the hospital would have been buried. The cemetery originally contained markers for the graves of twenty children, but today only one marker remains.

The administration building, now referred to as the "Main House," is the home to the first of many ghostly tales that have circulated among the

The former administration building of the Glenn Home. Fraternity brothers have experienced odd encounters inside the building. *Courtesy of Elizabeth Christjansen.*

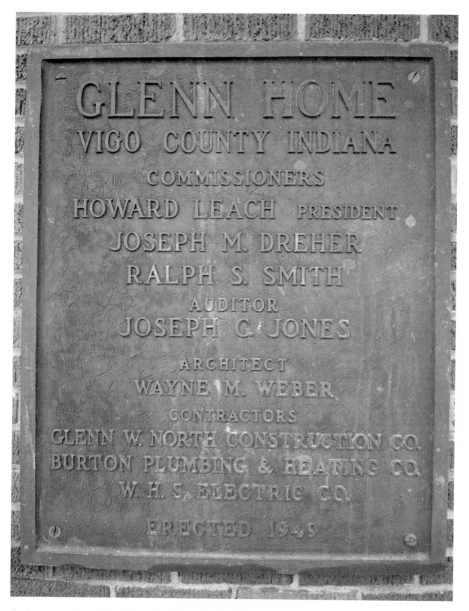

A plaque on the side of the administration building at the Glenn Home. *Courtesy of Elizabeth Christjansen.*

fraternity brothers over the years. As the story goes, a brother was living in a room on the second story of the Main House. On one particular evening, he found himself alone in the house. He soon heard knocking at the front door, but when he went to answer it, no one was there. Not really thinking it was anything strange, he headed back to his room. A while later, he heard the knocking again. He went downstairs to answer the door to find that again no one was there. He stepped outside to survey the area but saw no one. He headed back up to his room, at this point probably thinking he was the subject of a prank by his fellow brothers. When the knocking started again, he went back to answer the door. He must have been very bothered at this point because there was still no one there.

The student stepped outside but could not see a source for the mysterious knocking. He walked around the entire building but found himself alone on the property. Returning to the interior of the Main House, he was about to walk back upstairs to his room when he heard the knocking again. It was only then that he realized the knocking wasn't coming from the front door. The sound that had eluded him all evening was actually coming from a door located underneath the stairs. The student, quite spooked by this encounter, ran back to his room and locked the door. The room beneath the stairs was small, much like a storage closet, and contained only a radiator and a window. The location of the strange room and the unexplained knocking have led many of the brothers to believe that it could have been used as a "timeout/punishment room" for the children at the Glenn Home.

A little girl has also reportedly been encountered by brothers living in the Main House. She is said to appear in both windows and mirrors. Witnesses often just glimpse the girl, at first thinking they may be seeing their own reflection, but upon taking a second look they realize that it is the face of a child staring back at them. Items have been seen moving on their own, and things have been known to fall from secure locations with no apparent cause. The voice of a child has been heard in different areas throughout the house. Most who have encountered it state that it sounded like a young girl. The voice is not entirely audible, and the brothers have been unable to decipher the words. One incident involves brothers trying to provoke the spirit they referred to as Imogene. At the time of this encounter, the room the boys were in had a dimmer light switch, allowing the illumination of the room to be easily manipulated. They had closed the door to avoid being bothered by any outside sources or sounds. As they

The renovated Alden dormitory at the Glenn Home. *Courtesy of Elizabeth Christjansen.*

The condemned Leach dormitory at the Glenn Home. *Courtesy of Elizabeth Christjansen.*

A Bible scripture next to the door on the Leach dormitory. *Courtesy of Elizabeth Christjansen.*

sat in the dark discussing Imogene and their disbelief in her existence, they requested that the ghost prove to them that she existed. Imogene immediately responded, turning the dimmer switch all the way on, bathing the frightened boys in bright light. They looked for any explanation for the encounter, but with the door being shut and all brothers accounted for at the time the lights came on, it was hard for them to explain it as anything other than a visit from Imogene.

Another interesting story about the Main House comes from its early days as a rental. The home was initially rented by the fraternity in unfinished condition, so there was a bit of work to be done. A temporary wall with a door had been placed on the second floor, blocking the last two rooms in that area. Two brothers are reported to have entered that area and discovered what they believed to be a cage door with a feeding slot. They did not investigate the area further. Though no ghostly tales have been reported in that section of the house, the existence of the two strange rooms is rather puzzling.

Adjacent to the Main House is the former location of the Glenn Home pool, which is now a parking lot for the fraternity. Though this site has not been used as a pool for many years, it has been said that a female student crossing the parking lot one evening was shocked to hear the sound of children splashing and playing in that area. Obviously, there were no children on the grounds, so there was no obvious explanation for what the student heard.

Two of the Glenn Home's three dormitories are located next to the parking lot. They stand in stark contrast to each other as Alden was renovated in 2010. The building now serves as a chapter room, dining room and formal kitchen for the brothers, and its layout remains mostly the same from its earlier days as a dormitory. Leach, on the other hand, has suffered from years of abandonment. The building is weathered, and the foundation is cracked. The fraternity has boarded up the building due to safety concerns. One of these two dormitories is home to the next strange story of the Glenn Home. Because the story was first reported in 2005—prior to the renovation of Alden—it is hard to determine which dormitory was host to the encounter.

The students involved reported they were driving into the parking lot one evening when the headlights of the vehicle focused on the front door of one of the dormitories. The door to the building seemed to open and then close by itself. It was a windless evening, so the students found this to be rather strange. Upon returning to the dormitory later with friends, the students were shocked to discover that the door did not open in the same way they had witnessed earlier. What they had seen would have been going against the normal direction of the door's hinges. It has also been reported that the moans of sick or abused children can be heard in one of the dormitories. The burned remains of the former dormitory for African American youth are said to give students a strange feeling, though nothing has been reported in that area.

The remaining dormitory is called Owen, and it is likely the most haunted location on the former grounds of the Glenn Home. According to maps, this is also the dormitory that is likely closest to the old children's cemetery, which appears to be located in the woods somewhere between Owen and the dormitory for African American children. The fraternity currently uses Owen as a sort of multi-purpose area. The first floor of the building now includes a wood shop and rooms that can be used for fraternity parties and events. The upper floor houses a bar and stage as well as additional party rooms. The walls have been graffitied by current and former students, adding an abandoned feel to the highly frequented building. Several years ago, the fraternity even hosted a haunted house on the first floor of Owen, and those who survived the haunted house were rewarded with a Halloween party on the second floor.

The second floor of Owen is also home to the most widely circulated story of a ghostly encounter at the former Glenn Home. Years ago, brothers would store their belongings on the second floor of the building,

The burned remains of the dormitory for African American children. *Courtesy of Elizabeth Christjansen.*

and apparently a former brother had done just that during a break at Rose-Hulman. He had returned to the property early and was feeling tired. Rather than move his bed back into the Main House, he decided to spend the night in Owen. He would report later that sometime during the night, he was awakened by a rather strange sight. A young boy was sitting at the end of his bed. His first response was to be frightened of what he was seeing, but then the child began to speak to him. The brother must have calmed down at this point because he allowed the boy to tell him the story of another boy who was hiding in the hallway. The boy stated that the other child was "not very nice and always angry." The brother stated that while the child told him about the other boy, he was sure he heard something moving around in the hallway. After the encounter the brother fell back asleep, but the experience stuck with him. So much so that he would later research the history of the Glenn Home, focusing on the Owen dormitory. It is said that he found a record of two boys who once lived in Owen Hall long before the fraternity purchased the property. They were about the same age as the child who visited him.

The Owen dormitory at the Glenn Home. *Courtesy of Elizabeth Christjansen.*

The haunted hallway in the Owen dormitory. The spirits of two boys are thought to wander this area. *Courtesy of Elizabeth Christjansen.*

The boys had committed suicide by hanging themselves in Owen. I could find no record of any suicides in the Glenn Home, but with the rumors of abuse and the long history of the facility, one has to assume that the ghosts of these young boys have remained on the site due to trauma. The brother made several nighttime visits to Owen and continued to communicate with the friendlier of the two ghost children. During these encounters, he would hear strange sounds in the hallway as if a child were running around.

Owen is also the home to a ghost girl that is believed to have been a former resident of the Glenn Home. It is thought that she may have been killed while living in Owen and that her ghost remains there to this day. Former brothers have reported seeing the girl on multiple occasions. Windows have also been known to open on their own at Owen. One evening, following a party, one of the brothers entered Owen and closed all of the windows in the building. As he was walking back to the Main House, he happened to turn around to glance back at Owen. He was shocked to see that every window he had just closed was open once again. Needless to say, he was so terrified that he refused to reenter the building to close the windows. No other brothers entered the building that night, and the windows remained open until the following morning. It is reported that there were several witnesses to this event.

The Glenn Home is also rumored to have a connection to notorious cult leader Charles Manson. Though Charles Manson was born in Cincinnati, he spent quite a bit of time in Indiana during his early years, though mostly in boarding schools for difficult and defiant children. Manson was a troubled youth, committing petty crimes from as early an age as ten. In 1947 when Charles was just thirteen, he was sent to the Gibault School for Boys in Terre Haute. The institution was operated by Roman Catholic priests, who were known for being very strict and using wooden paddles and leather straps on disobedient students. During Manson's stay at Gibault, it is believed that he could have made his way to the Glenn Home—either as a resident or as a participant in events that might have included both Gibault and the Glenn Home. Manson ran away from Gibault on at least two occasions and would later become a frequent resident of the Indiana Boy's School in Plainfield.

In the years since the Glenn Home closed its doors, reports of ghostly activity seem to be a common occurrence. With so much history and so many people passing through the home, it's possible that something otherworldly is occurring at the former Glenn Home. Perhaps the spectral inhabitants of the home are making themselves known or possibly there is residual energy of horrendous acts that may have occurred there. Regardless, it is likely that the tales of strange activity will continue at the Glenn Home, and the brothers of Pi Kappa Alpha will continue to keep the stories alive.

CONCLUSION

Though Terre Haute may not be the most haunted town in the Midwest, it does have its fair share of ghost stories and local legends. As the fascination with the supernatural seems to grow thanks to books, television shows, blogs and podcasts, Terre Haute's haunted history is also seeing a revival. The Vigo County Historical Society will be devoting a section to local myths and legends at its new location in the former Erhmann Manufacturing building—once known as the Glidden building at Ninth Street and Wabash Avenue. Stiffy Green will be overseeing the area, welcoming visitors to the museum. The little bulldog has also gained new notoriety in the city. A local brewing company has named a beer in his honor complete with a can adorned with his wrinkly, green-eyed face.

Terre Haute is also home to Dead Zone Paranormal Radio, certainly the first radio show of its kind in Terre Haute. The Vigo County Historical Society hosts a Time Travelers' Club, giving locals a glimpse into some of Terre Haute's historic and unique buildings and locations. One has to wonder how many of those old buildings could house the spirits of Terre Haute's early inhabitants. The Haunted History Walking Tour of Downtown Terre Haute currently takes patrons on an adventure through the dark and ghostly history of the city. With so much interest in otherworldly activity, perhaps one day soon Terre Haute will be able to fully reclaim its early roots as a Spiritualist haven and embrace the spirits that remain from the city's past.

BIBLIOGRAPHY

Andrews, Ronald. "History of Markle's Mill." *Ronald Andrews* (blog), May 21, 1973. http://www.randrews4.com.

Arceo, Austin. "Tales of Hauntings Passed Down at Rose-Hulman's Fraternity House." *Tribune Star*, October 28, 2007. https://www.tribstar.com.

Asylum Projects. "Cottage Planned Institutions." *Asylum Projects Reserve Preteritus*. Accessed February 2019. http://www.asylumprojects.org.

Baker, Ronald L. *Hoosier Folk Legends*. Bloomington: Indiana University Press, 1982.

Biel, John G. "The Story of a House." *Terre Haute Saturday Spectator*, February 18, 1920.

Briseno, Danny. "Dignity Brought to Sin City." *Prairie Press Paris Beacon-News*, April 24, 2017. http://www.prairiepress.net.

Brown, Garett. "Bicentennial Celebration: The Mill and House Markle Built." *WTHITV*, April 26, 2018. https://www.wthitv.com.

Clark, Dorothy J. "Markle Park Establishment Causes Renewed Interest." *Terre Haute Tribune Star*, February 11, 1968.

Collier, Don. "Burford Renovations Done." *The Sycamore*, August 18, 2006. https://www.isustudentmedia.com.

Find A Grave. "Anna Reiss, Memorial No. 77443438." *Wabash Valley Genealogy Society Cemetery Committee*. Accessed February 2019. https://www.findagrave.com.

———. "Anna M. Reiss, Memorial No. 343442035." *Wabash Valley Genealogy Society Cemetery Committee*. Accessed February 2019. https://www.findagrave.com.

———. "Blackford Mill Condit, Memorial No. 27363574." *Wabash Valley Genealogy Society Cemetery Committee*. Accessed January 2019. https://www.findagrave.com.

———. "Caroline Reiss, Memorial No. 34342036." *Wabash Valley Genealogy Society Cemetery Committee*. Accessed February 2019. https://www.findagrave.com.

———. "Claude Herbert, Memorial No. 163586419." *Wabash Valley Genealogy Society Cemetery Committee*. Accessed February 2019. https://www.findagrave.com.

———. "Emma Condit, Memorial No. 27363578." *Wabash Valley Genealogy Society Cemetery Committee*. Accessed January 2019. https://www.findagrave.com.

———. "Emma Reiss, Memorial No. 40651077." *Wabash Valley Genealogy Society Cemetery Committee*. Accessed February 2019. https://www.findagrave.com.

———. "Frederick Markle, Memorial No. 30917120." *Wabash Valley Genealogy Society Cemetery Committee*. Accessed January 2019. https://www.findagrave.com.

———. "Gottlieb Reiss, Memorial No. 40651078." *Wabash Valley Genealogy Society Cemetery Committee*. Accessed February 2019. https://www.findagrave.com.

———. "Helen Condit, Memorial No. 27363579." *Wabash Valley Genealogy Society Cemetery Committee*. Accessed January 2019. https://www.findagrave.com.

———. "Howe Allen Condit, Memorial No. 27363580." *Wabash Valley Genealogy Society Cemetery Committee*. Accessed January 2019. https://www.findagrave.com.

———. "Ida Finkelstein, Memorial No. 13559278." *Wabash Valley Genealogy Society Cemetery Committee*. Accessed February 2019. https://www.findagrave.com.

———. "John C. Reiss, Memorial No. 77443252." *Wabash Valley Genealogy Society Cemetery Committee*. Accessed February 2019. https://www.findagrave.com.

———. "John G. Heinl, Memorial No. 3773." *Wabash Valley Genealogy Society Cemetery Committee*. Accessed December 2018. https://www.findagrave.com.

———. "Reverend Blackford Condit, Memorial No. 27363575." *Wabash Valley Genealogy Society Cemetery Committee*. Accessed January 2019. https://www.findagrave.com.

———. "Rosa K. Dedert, Memorial No. 36632314." *Wabash Valley Genealogy Society Cemetery Committee*. Accessed February 2019. https://www.findagrave.com.

———. "Sarah Louisa Condit, Memorial No. 27363581." *Wabash Valley Genealogy Society Cemetery Committee*. Accessed January 2019. https://www.findagrave.com.

———. "Sr Theodore Guerin, Memorial No. 14789822." *Wabash Valley Genealogy Society Cemetery Committee*. Accessed December 2018. https://www.findagrave.com.

Fink, John F. "Mother Theodore Guerin: Indiana's Very Own Saint." *Franciscan Media*. https://www.franciscanmedia.org.

Foulkes, Arthur. "Legend, Mystery, Folklore Part of Ghost Walk at ISU." *Tribune Star*, May 2, 2011. https://www.tribstar.com.

Francis, Judy. "A Look Back at the Dewees-Preston-Smith House at 13½ and Poplar." *Terre Haute Tribune Star*, July 5, 2015.

Haunted Legends in and around the Wabash Valley. "The Headless Trainman." Angelfire. Accessed February 2019. http://www.angelfire.com.

Haunted Places. "Markle Mill–Old Mill Dam." Accessed January 2019. https://www.hauntedplaces.org.

Higgins, Alvin M. "Howe Allen Condit." *Saturday Spectator*, February 22, 1935.

Hopkins, Marjorie. "Legends of the Valley." *Terre Haute Tribune Star*, October 13, 2013. https://www.tribstar.com.

How It Works. "What Are Blue Holes?" February 1, 2014. https://www.howitworksdaily.com.

Hughes, Frances E. "Mystery Surround Terre Haute Landmark." *Terre Haute Spectator*, December 22, 1979.

Hunter, Al. "Charles Manson—Hoosier Juvenile Delinquent." *Weekly View*, November 30, 2017. http://weeklyview.net.

———. "Gypsy Ghosts in Terry Hot." *Weekly View*, May 15, 2014. http://weeklyview.net.

Indiana Haunted Houses. "Real Haunts in Terre Haute—Old Mill Dam." Accessed January 2019. https://www.indianahauntedhouses.com.

Indiana Historical Bureau. "Markle Mill Site." Accessed January 2019. https://www.in.gov.

Indiana Landmarks. "Markle House." Accessed January 2019. https://www.indianalandmarks.org.

———. "Normal Hall Inspires Again." September 6, 2016. Accessed February 2019.

Indiana State University. "Condit House." Accessed January 2019. www.indstate.edu.

Jerse, Dorothy Weinz. *On This Day in Terre Haute History*. Charleston, SC: The History Press, 2015.

Landmark Hunter. "House at 823 Ohio Street." Accessed February 2019. http://landmarkhunter.com.

Leigh, Veronica. "Sin City i.e. Terre Haute, Indiana." *Confessions of an Author* (blog), June 13, 2016. http://veronicaleigh.blogspot.com.

Litchford, Heather. "Terre Haute Crossroads of America—Markle Mill." Accessed January 2019. http://heatherlitchford.blogspot.com.

Malach, Maggie. "Ghosts Might Attend These 7 Supposedly Haunted Colleges and Universities." *Mental Floss*, October 27, 2015. http://mentalfloss.com.

Malone, Dave. "Tales from the Campus Crypt." *State, the Magazine of Indiana State University*, October 1, 2014. http://statemagazine.com.

McCormick, Mike. "Anna M. Stewart Gains Notoriety for Her Communication with the Dead." *Terre Haute Tribune Star*, May 20, 2001.

———. "The Story of Two Homicides, Part One." *Terre Haute Tribune Star*, February 18, 2001.

———. "The Story of Two Homicides, Part Two." *Terre Haute Tribune Star*, February 25, 2001.

———. "Terre Haute: Queen City of the Wabash." Charleston, SC: Arcadia Publishing, 2005.

———. "Wabash Valley Profile—John G. Heinl." *Wabash Valley Visions and Voices*, November 17, 2005. http://visions.indstate.edu.

———. "Wabash Valley Profile—Levi G. Warren." *Wabash Valley Visions and Voices*, February 24, 2002. http://visions.indstate.edu.

———. "Wabash Valley Profile—Markle's Mill." *Wabash Valley Visions and Voices*, August 14, 2016. http://visions.indstate.edu.

Mitchell, Dawn. "Retro Indy: Charles Manson, Mass Murderer and Cult Leader, Spent Time in Indiana." *Indianapolis Star*, January 14, 2014. https://www.indystar.com.

Mount Carmel Daily Republican. "Student Dies While Surfing." March 21, 1991.

National Register of Historic Places. Condit House nomination form. October 2, 1972. https://npgallery.nps.gov.

―――. Vigo County Home for Dependent Children registration form. May 18, 2000. https://npgallery.nps.gov.

Nick, Tanis. "Historical Treasure Santa Tried to Save Everyone in Horrific TH Fire in 1898." *Terre Haute Tribune Star,* December 16, 2018. https://www.tribstar.com.

Patrick, Linda. "Indiana State Normal School 150 Years and Counting." *Tribune Star*, November 22, 2015. https://www.tribstar.com.

―――. "Round Stone, Light Have Unique History." *Terre Haute Tribune Star*, November 30, 2003.

Reynolds, Bluke. "League of Women Voters Tries to Save Glenn Home." *Pi Kappa Alpha*, 2016. https://www.pi-kappa-alpha.net.

―――. "1973 Status of the Glenn Home License." *Pi Kappa Alpha*, 2016. https://www.pi-kappa-alpha.net.

Saint Mary-of-the-Woods College. "Quick Facts about Saint Mother Theodore Guerin." Accessed December 2018. https://spsmw.org.

―――. "Saint Mother Theodore Guerin Miracle Storied Contributed to Sainthood." Accessed December 2018. https://spsmw.org.

―――. "Saint Mother Theodore Guerin's Story." Accessed December 2018. https://spsmw.org.

―――. "Steps to Sainthood." Accessed December 2018. https://spsmw.org.

―――　"White Violet Center for Eco-Justice." Accessed December 2018. https://spsmw.org.

Sarkar, Dipa. "Glenn Home Helped Children for Many Years." *Tribune Star*, September 23, 2006. https://www.tribstar.com.

Smith, Hannah. "Ghosts Haunt Students Footsteps." *Indiana Statesman*, October 29, 2010. https://www.isustudentmedia.com.

Terre Haute Saturday Spectator. "Chat." August 23, 1940.

―――. "Death Notice of Chapman J. Root." November 30, 1945.

―――. "Death Notice of Howe Allen Condit." February 22, 1935.

―――. "Death Notice of Martin Sheets." March 5, 1926.

―――. "Death Notice of Susan Sheets." May 10, 1929.

―――. "Funeral Services for C.J. Root Held Friday, Nationally Known as Great Industrialist." November 23, 1945.

―――."Obituary of Miss Helen Condit." December 15, 1961.

―――. "Personal and Society." August 5, 1932.

―――. "Society Page." August 18, 1928.

―――. "Tomb Telephones." April 3, 1926.

Terre Haute Tribune. "George Dewees." June 2, 1973.

———. "Glenn Home." May 29, 1975.

———. "Problems Grow at the Glenn Home." June 28, 1973.

———. "Rites Wednesday for Mrs. Burford." July 6, 1970.

Terre Haute Tribune Star. "ISTC Will Dedicate New Hall; Honor Former Deans." October 18, 1959.

———. "Riverton Parke Class Visit Highland Lawn Cemetery." April 26, 2012. https://www.tribstar.com.

TerrorHaute. "Martin Sheets." Accessed December 2018. http://www.terrorhaute.com.

Trigg, Lisa. "Downed Trees in River Threaten Markle Mill." *Terre Haute Tribune Star*, August 13, 2013. https://www.tribstar.com.

———. "Markle Mill among State's Low-head." *Dam Dangerous Sites*, April 3, 2017. https://www.tribstar.com.

United States American History. "History of Terre Haute." Accessed December 2018. https://www.u-s-history.com.

Vigo County Historical Society. "Local Legends." Accessed December 2018. https://www.vchsmuseum.org.

ABOUT THE AUTHOR

Ashley Hood is the owner and tour guide of Tell-Tale Tours, a haunted history walking tour business in her hometown of Terre Haute, Indiana. She has been fascinated with the history of haunted locations and the "things that go bump in the night" since early childhood, often exploring local cemeteries and haunted bridges in rural Indiana as a teenager. In the years since, Ashley has conducted paranormal investigations throughout the midwestern United States, visiting some of the Midwest's most haunted locations. She is a collector of all things macabre and unusual and loves to visit strange and unique locations. She also writes two blogs for the Tell-Tale Tours website. The *Tell-Tale Traveler* highlights her odd, sometimes morbid and often haunted travels. The other blog, called the *Graveyard Verses*, features the history and haunts of cemeteries that she has visited. Ashley resides in Terre Haute, Indiana, with a family of fur babies, and yes, she is a crazy cat lady.

Visit us at
www.historypress.com